Angling Times

Yearbook 1979~80

Editor Peter Maskell

Art Editor David Weaver

Published by Macdonald & Jane's Publishers Ltd,
Paulton House, 8 Shepherdess Walk, London N1 7LW, in association with
EMAP National Publications Ltd, 21 Church Walk, Peterborough, PE1 2TW.

Set and Composed by CALL Printers Ltd, Cambridge & St. Ives.
Colour process by Woolthame Ltd, London EC3.
Printed in Great Britain by Hazell, Watson and Viney, Aylesbury

Limp edition: ISBN 0354 090933
Cased edition: ISBN 0354 090925

Introduction

by Barry Dennis
Editor of Angling Times

ANGLING still reigns supreme as the country's biggest participant sport with hundreds of people, both young and old, picking up a rod for the first time every year. Every angler remembers the excitement of hooking and landing that first fish.

Big or small that first fish gets the adrenalin flowing. Is it a British record or a minnow? That's what fishing is all about — never knowing what to expect next.

All the excitement of the last 12 months is captured in words and pictures in the 1979/80 Angling Times Yearbook. Young or old, beginner or expert you will find that it deserves a place on your bookshelf.

Once again we feature coarse fishing, match fishing, sea fishing and stillwater trout fishing but one very important new addition this year is more instructional material. In fact we think you will find it almost as exciting as actual fishing. Good reading and happy fishing!

Contents

Coarse Fishing

by Peter Maskell

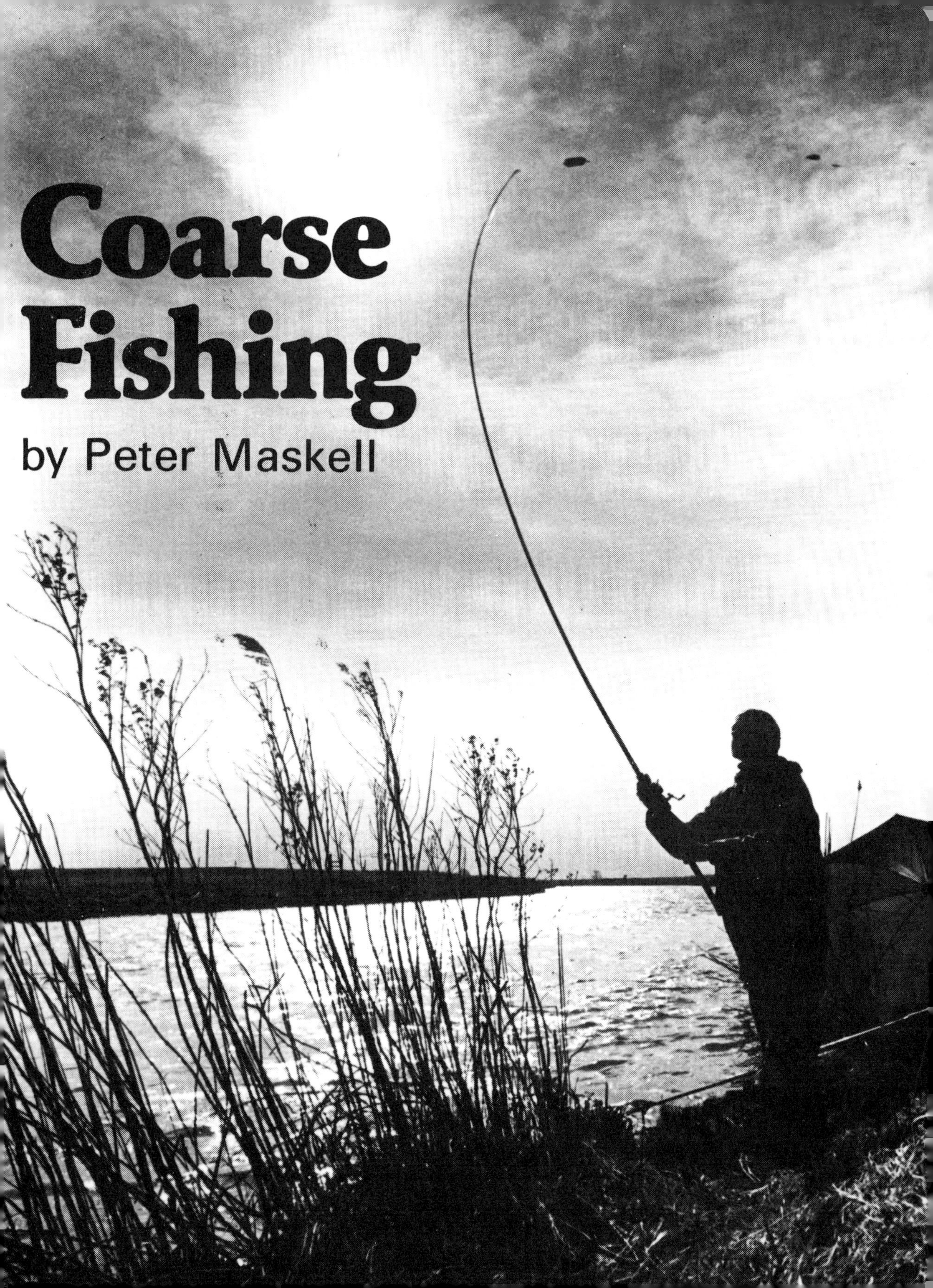

Coarse Fishing

For the majority of Britain's two million coarse anglers the last 12 months have been far from impressive. The standard of sport, in any given year, is dependent on a variety of factors — most of which are beyond the angler's control.

The last year has clearly demonstrated the vital effect played by our unpredictable climate on the feeding habits of our coarse fish — and the result was a short season and thousands of frustrated anglers.

The opening months of the 1978/79 season saw temperatures below seasonal average. Rainfall was heavier than normal too. Autumn brought some unexpected consolation in the form of several weeks of dry, unusually warm weather. But, unfortunately, this was soon followed by one of the worst winters on record with temperatures below zero and heavy falls of snow.

The last three months of the coarse fishing season were simply frozen off. Many major venues were unfishable for weeks on end and, even when the weather eased temporarily, there were few anglers about to take advantage of the conditions.

But it would be unfair to label the season as one of the worst on record. Large catches of fish, and catches of large fish, were made regularly even though some areas of the country produced far better sport than others.

A thorough study of the records shows that the season was above average as far as catches of big tench were concerned. Tench are essentially one of the mainstay species of the opening 10 or 12 weeks of any new season. And the 1978/79 season produced some of the most exciting catches of all time.

Literally dozens of 6 and 7lb fish were reported from dozens of different venues. Anglers have at last come to appreciate the tremendous potential offered by the network of gravel pits, dotted throughout the country. With river sport increasingly unpredictable more and more anglers are turning to stillwaters for their fishing, especially during the summer months.

The top specimen hunters have also recognised the potential of gravel pits — especially the huge gravel workings in the Home Counties. The persistence of these top anglers has clearly paid off in catch returns and the familiar names of these anglers, men like Phil Smith of Coventry, Kevin Clifford of Yorkshire and Mike Voller of Watford are cropping up time and again.

A single session at Harefield pits in Middlesex produced fish of 7lb 12oz, 7lb 10oz and 7lb 2oz for Mike Voller — superb sport by any yardstick.

The top ten lists for bream and roach also indicate that, as far as specimen fish were concerned, the season was certainly above average. Yet it remains a fact that the majority of anglers are not concerned with specimens. They measure the success of a season by the number of times they fish and manage to catch perhaps a couple of pounds of small fish.

In this respect the season was certainly poorer than average. The majority of anglers rely on our major rivers for their sport — and these waterways face the constant pressures of pollution and abstraction as well as the vagaries of climate.

None of the major rivers fished well, and catch returns certainly didn't reflect the vast stocks of fish which inhabit these rivers. The Severn produced good sport in the summer and autumn but was virtually unfishable in winter.

The River Thames, perhaps the finest mixed fishery in the country, was equally poor. Top anglers struggled for a few pounds of fish at the top venues on the river and the catches of the pleasure anglers were even lower.

Only the Trent managed to salvage its reputation, although it was badly hit by sudden floods caused by melting snow in the Derbyshire hills. By Trent standards the river performed badly, but in the general context of British river fishing it was easily the most consistent venue.

The worst hit area of all was Eastern England. The slow moving rivers, the Welland and Nene, and the network of narrow drains fished terribly. There were outcries from anglers about the poor quality of sport but tests by the Anglian Water Authority proved that there was little wrong with the density of fish stocks in these waters.

The problem was, of course, water temperature. The colder the water the less the fish move about. They expend less energy and therefore need to eat less food to keep their metabolisms ticking over. The end result, as far as the angler is concerned, is fewer bites and fewer fish in the net at the end of the day.

Under adverse weather condtiions an angler may fail to get a single bite from a swim which is packed with fish in a semi-dormant state. This state of affairs may be frustrating for the angler but he does at least have the consolation of knowing that there is nothing drastically wrong with the fish stocks themselves. An improvement in water temperature is all that is needed to galvanise the fish into feeding again.

Although tackle, tactics and the general standard of angling continues to improve each year the angler cannot hope to control the weather.

A fine opening month catch of tench taken from a Midland brick pit.

Zander

In the past decade, no freshwater record has tumbled as often as that for the zander. Indeed, since July 1968, when the standard was set by an 8lb 8¼oz fish from Woburn, the British Record (Rod Caught) Fish Committee has accepted claims for no fewer than ten heavier zander.

Of these fish, all but one — and that a Woburn fish from the early days — has come from the Great Ouse Relief Channel in Norfolk. This was the water into which the original Fenland stocking was made in March 1963. All subsequent record fish have been either these original stock, or their descendants.

On the face of it, then, no record should be easier to crack. The Relief Channel, patently the obvious venue, is fishable on a day or season permit available to everybody. Although the channel is eleven miles long, it is inevitable that when a spate of large fish is caught, news gets out to the extent where a would-be record cracker can have an approximate idea of the shoal's locality (zander being pack fish). And the actual technique of catching zander is simplicity itself.

But a look at the table of record zander shows a spate of big fish between 10lb and 12lb-plus in the period 1968 to 1971, followed by something of a milestone catch by Bill Chillingworth. His 15lb 5oz fish, taken from the channel in February 1971, was to stand almost unchallenged for over six years.

Only then was there an indication that another fish bettering that weight was still there for the catching. Steve Smith, captor of a mighty 16lb 6oz fish from the neighbouring Cut Off Channel, made one 'fatal' error in that he returned the zander to the water after its capture in October 1976. As a result, despite the fish having been weighed on two sets of scales, his claim was not accepted by the record committee.

Soon after, Norfolk angler Ralph Younge took a zander of 15lb 6¼oz from the Relief Channel, and this time the fish was knocked on the head. Whatever the morality of it, the committee was quite willing to accept it as the new British Record, despite it weighing less than Smith's fish.

Fortunately, the issue was soon put beyond doubt. Younge's angling partner Dave Litton, who had done the groundwork in locating the best swims, took a 17¼-pounder from virtually the same spot. That was in October 1977.

The 1978/79 season looked like being one when the zander record would tumble again and again . . . big fish appeared to be moving in the Relief Channel, and a new Water Authority by-law made it legal to fish for zander and pike from June 16 onwards. Yet Litton's fish still stands.

To understand this paradox, it is necessary to look at the growth rate related to the age of Relief Channel zander. It has been suggested that the lifespan of a zander is around 13 years, and to make maximum growth, these fish must have an uninterrupted and plentiful supply of food.

From their introduction in1963 up until 1971, the Relief Channel fulfilled this requirement perfectly. Then, for reasons which some attribute to the zander themselves and others blame on outside factors, the amount of food fish available fell off sharply and the channel zander began to go back in condition. If they did not actually lose weight, they were not maintaining their original gain of around 2lb a year, while at the same time they were approaching 'middle age'.

Bill Chillingworth's 15lb 5oz record would seem to be the heaviest of the original 97 stock fish, for in the following three years the nearest approaching that weight was a 14lb 2½oz specimen in 1972. It is now all but certain that the original zander have died of old age.

To find the zander which came on the scene to topple Chillingworth's fish, we must look to the second generation of Relief Channel fish. These were probably spawned in 1964/65 and, though they suffered through the same lean years as their parents, they were still young enough to benefit from the improved food supply which came along in 1975. So although they did not achieve the optimum growth rate, they grew big enough to take the record.

It now looks as though Dave Litton's 17¼-pounder filled the same ecological niche as Chillingworth's fish, being the last and largest of the line. But as each year goes by, there will be a bigger and bigger back-up population of zander from annual spawnings of its descendants.

The presence of a larger head of big, though not record-sized, zander will deal a blow to the chances of another Relief Channel record. The more competitors for a given amount of food, the less likelihood there is of any one of them reaching

Date	Weight
July 1968	8lb 8¼oz
August 1968	9lb
September 1968	9lb 2oz
November 1968	10lb 4oz
October 1969	10¾lb
February 1970	12lb 5oz
August 1970	12lb 6½oz
October 1970	12lb 13oz
February 1971	15lb 5oz
September 1977	15lb 6¼oz
October 1976	17¼lb

Top zander, 1978/79:

15lb 12oz, Relief Channel, August 1978; Lester Strudwick, Potter's Bar, Herts.
14lb 13oz, Fen drain, November 1978; Bryan Culley, Quorn, Leics.
14lb 10oz, Fen drain, October 1978; Alan Newcombe, Grantham, Lincs.
14lb 9oz, Relief Channel, September 1978; Trefor West, Coventry.
14lb 7oz, Relief Channel, August 1978; Paul Williams, Dudley, West Midlands.
13lb 4oz, Fen drain, August 1978; David Goodrum, Grantham, Lincs.
12lb 13oz, Fen drain, November 1978; Bryan Derrington, Birmingham.
12lb 2oz, Fen drain, November 1978; Alex Evans, Southport, Merseyside.
12lb 1oz, Cut Off Channel, March 1979; Geoff Loan, Swaffham, Norfolk.

This massive zander catch, totalling 129lb, was taken from the River Wissey in Norfolk.

Captor	Venue
J. Dickman	Woburn Abbey
A. Howe	Relief Channel
P. Bates	Woburn Abbey
R. Watcham	Relief Channel
M. Baker	Relief Channel
B. Rickards	Relief Channel
N. Fickling	Relief Channel
N. Fickling	Relief Channel
W. Chillingworth	Relief Channel
R. Younge	Relief Channel
D. Litton	Relief Channel

the target. And this assumes a steady supply of small food fish, which is a dangerous assumption.

What price, then, a record from another water? Ever since their introduction, zander have spread throughout the Fen network and now colonise the whole Middle Level system to a greater or lesser degree. Yet the waters that have turned up the best fish to date — the Cut-Off Channel, the Delph, the Old Bedford — are so closely tied up with the Relief Channel that their limitations are the same. The one stillwater to figure in the list, Roswell Pits, is connected to the Great Ouse and so shares in the problem of a declining food fish population. Regulars there will tell of fish falling away in condition.

The Fen drains at the fringe of the Middle Level network have yet to produce any sizeable zander, though small fish have shown in good numbers. The assumption to draw is that the younger the fish, the greater its wanderlust when food supplies become short. So although these pioneers are youthful, there could soon be a time when they will be record-contenders . . . assuming the food supply lasts.

There are other zander to consider, those introduced away from the Fens by so-called 'pirate' stockers. Ironically, these illegal travellers may hold the key to a future record.

It is certain zander have gone into the Thames, Severn and Warwickshire Avon. An angler who wishes to remain nameless assures us that there is not a major river in the country which does not hold the fish.

One swallow does not make a summer, but should a sufficient concentration of fish form to make a breeding population, then any river with a high population of bleak, small roach or similarly bite-sized fish could be the site of the next record.

How big is that fish likely to be? There is evidence that British zander could reach weights a little in excess of 20lb. And whatever your views of the fish, that's surely a sporting proposition!

Tactics for big bream

The meres of Cheshire and Shropshire have probably produced more big bream over the years than any other area in England, yet they remain virtually unfished. This stems from the fact that catching a 7lb plus bream from these waters is far from easy and requires a great deal of time and effort.

Many anglers soon lose interest after one or two fruitless visits, preferring venues where smaller fish can be caught more readily.

The difficulties encountered when fishing the meres for the first time are numerous but probably the two most important factors to overcome are:

Location. There are comparatively few fish for the size of water. Therefore, locating the bream shoals is absolutely vital. Failure to do this can mean many hours wasted, fishing areas that the bream never visit.

Natural Food. Many meres have a soft almost liquid mud bottom and this provides a perfect home for vast beds of bloodworm and other insect life. The hot, sunny days of summer can also cause acres of water to become alive with daphnia, drifting on the wind to every corner of the mere. With all this rich feeding readily available, it is plain to see why an angler's bait is easily missed. It is this abundance of natural food, however, that produces the specimen fish.

Here then lies the challenge — relatively few fish, feeding in small areas with a more than adequate food supply. The first steps to success should be spent finding an area that bream frequent. This can be narrowed down by a bream's fancies.

It is a fact that they very rarely feed close to the bank and are normally at least 25 yards out. They are also attracted by ledges, shelves and other irregular features on the bottom of the mere, especially if these are in 7-12 feet of water.

Start finding these contours and depths by careful plumbing, either from the bank or, better still, from a boat if this is allowed. The peculiar habit bream have of rolling or priming during feeding or when moving to a feeding area can be used to advantage. Always make a note of where, and at what time, they were seen, as this can quite often lead you to a hot spot.

After finding a likely feeding area, the next task is preparing the swim. There are no secret or exotic baits as far as bream are concerned — maggots, worms and bread are all that is needed. What is necessary, however, is to introduce the selected bait into the swim as often as possible.

This means mid-week baiting trips as well as baiting-up prior to fishing. A typical groundbaiting consists of 8-10lb of brown groundbait (this blends in with the dark mud much better than white and there is less chance of alarming the fish) two pints of maggots and 50 chopped worms.

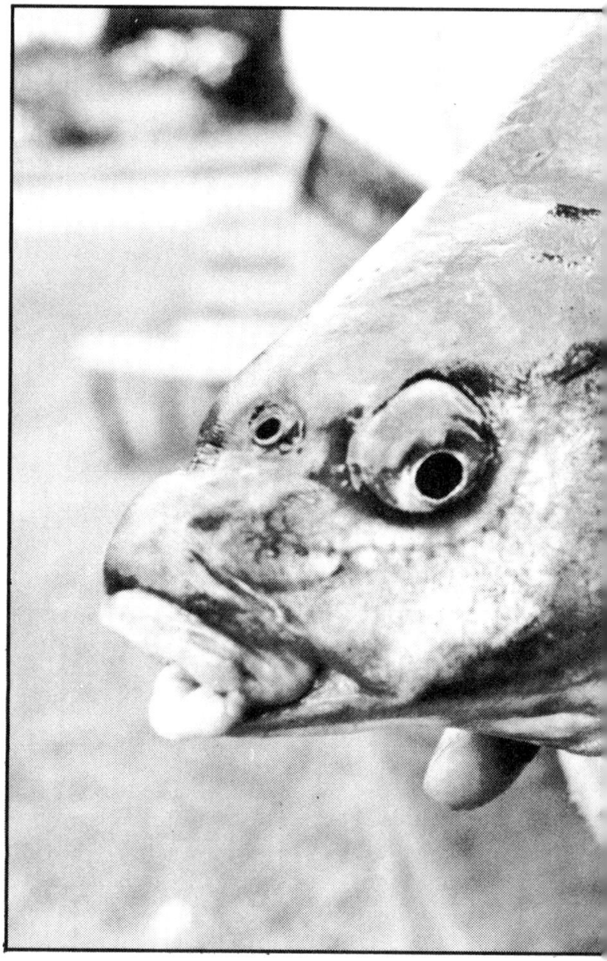

If bread is the hookbait then substitute some of the maggots and worms with bread pellets. This continual feeding in one area will, hopefully, become part of the mere's food supply as far as the bream are concerned and the chances of them sampling your hookbait are greatly increased.

Because of the distances at which bream are encountered, 95% of fishing time is spent legering. As most of the meres have very soft bottoms, it is important that your hookbait is not buried in the mud.

The two old established methods of paternoster or long link leger rigs will overcome this, but what

by Roger Harker

Face to face with one of those elusive specimen bream. Follow the simple rules and results will follow, provided the angler is patient and prepared to persevere at a selected water.

you can do is double your chances by fishing two hook rigs, either two paternosters or one paternoster and a long link. I am surprised more anglers do not do this, as it has certainly helped me catch more fish over the years.

Bream are not renowned for their fighting ability and this is generally true of the bigger ones. Therefore, my reel line is no more than 5lb b.s. with 3 or 4lb b.s. hook lengths. A 12 foot fast taper hollow glass rod completes the set up.

For bite indication I place my faith in a glow-bobbin indicator in conjunction with a buzzer, while others prefer a swing tip or butt indicator. All these methods have proved themselves so choose a method that you have most confidence in. Bites are normally confident, starting with a couple of one inch lifts followed by a steady pull towards the butt ring. As it reaches the butt ring the strike is made.

It is impossible to generalise on feeding times, as they can vary so much from one water to another. On one mere I fish, the bream can be expected from 11.00pm until 2.00am returning for a short spell just after dawn. While on another water just two miles away, there is virtually no action at night, the best time being from 11.00am to 1.00pm.

It is true to say, however, that once these feeding patterns have been established then the bream in those waters will more often than not be in that area during those times.

Having said this, however, always be prepared for the unexpected, bream have a habit of shattering the most well founded theories. Do not expect big bags of bream from the meres, one fish in a typical session from Friday evening until Sunday afternon is rated as fishing well, so be prepared for long blank periods.

These lean spells are more likely to increase in July and August when the food supply is at its greatest, and decrease in September and October as the food chain starts dying.

There are certainly no short cuts to success on the meres.

Top bream, 1978/79:

12lb 4oz, Wilstone reservoir, Tring, August 1978; Richard Reader, Hemel Hempstead.
11lb 13oz, Startops reservoir, Tring, June 1978; John Howe, Chesham, Bucks.
11lb 8oz, Staffs Mere, July 1978; Alan Griffiths, Stone, Staffs.
11lb 5oz, Staffs Mere, July 1978; Mike Hurst, Stoke-on-Trent.
10lb 8oz, Wilstone reservoir, Tring, August 1978; Paul Mardle, Luton, Beds.
10lb 6oz, Tring reservoirs, Herts, August 1978; Phil Large, Dunstable, Beds.
10lb 6oz, Castle Ashby Lakes, Northampton, October 1978; Brett Marshall, Northampton.
10lb 4oz, Wilstone reservoir, Tring, July 1978; Peter Frost, Dunstable, Beds.
10lb 2oz, Lake at Harefield, Middlesex, July 1978; Peter Lambert, South Harrow.
10lb 2oz, Tring reservoirs, Herts, October 1978; Colin Kingham, Flitwick, Beds.

Pike

The 1978/79 pike season was a season of qualified success. No fewer than a dozen fish topping the 30lb mark were reported, despite one of the worst winters since the freeze-up of 1963.

Considering that the last three months of the season were either washed out or frozen off by the weather, results were remarkably good. Had conditions been a little kinder and the final three months, traditionally the best of every pike season, fishable at the major venues, the season might well have been one of the best on record.

Even so a dozen fish, topping the 30lb mark, were recorded. And while none of them came anywhere near threatening the existing British record, results were at least comparable with the previous two seasons.

Seven of the top ten fish were taken from stillwaters, as far apart as Kent and Cheshire. There is little doubt that gravel pits and lakes, spared from the twin evils of pollution and abstraction, offer the best chance of a potential record breaker.

But, by an interesting contrast, the season also threw up three tremendous river pike from quite different rivers. A 31½lb fish was taken from the River Wye, a water largely untapped in terms of coarse fish potential.

Because this particular river holds a large head of salmon the water quality has not deteriorated drastically during the last decade and the future of its coarse fish stocks is closely allied with the quality of the game fishing.

The river contains a reasonable head of big pike and its potential remains largely untapped. Although a 30 pounder may seem impressive it's a fair bet that the river holds much larger specimens — fish that would soon show in catch returns if the river were subjected to the same kind of pressures as the narrow Fen waterways.

Matching that Wye catch in terms of significance were two other river fish. The larger, a 32lb specimen, fell in October and was taken from the Ure at Boroughbridge. A pike of these proportions is sensational for any river — let alone those in the Yorkshire river system.

Yet reports from other anglers have indicated a sudden upsurge in the stocks of smaller fish in the Yorkshire rivers and the coarse fishing prospects in this traditionally dour region are looking as promising as at any time in the last decade.

A 32lb pike from a Yorkshire river is the equivalent of a 42lb fish from a stillwater and is, perhaps, an indication that the existing British record of 40lb is by no means an unobtainable target.

The third massive river fish was taken from the River Kennet at Kintbury, Wilts. The Kennet has far more in common with the Wye than the Ure.

It is a relatively unpolluted river, supporting big shoals of barbel and chub and a water long respected for its specimen potential. Pike anglers, by and large, concentrate on stillwaters and the narrow Fenland drains.

The capture of these three massive river pike may, perhaps, divert the attentions of a few of them to the potential of our major rivers.

A sudden upsurge in angling concentration on our major rivers could well throw up some very interesting results.

Yet during the last decade there has been a definite trend towards the stillwaters and drains by the more enthusiastic pike anglers. The Fen drains — although still offering the best chance of a high double or 20 pounder — have definitely reached their peak.

These narrow waterways are not able to sustain the kind of angling pressure to which they have been subjected during the last decade.

Unless the drains are given some respite from angling pressure they will continue to decline. A

A leaping pike displays the aggressive power which makes the species a sporting quarry.

careful study of the results of the last three seasons indicate they offer little chance of turning up a 30 pounder.

In contrast the larger gravel pits, especially those in the South of England, continue to dominate the list of the largest pike of the season. Gravel pit fishing may require a technique of its own, but the rewards are there for all to see.

Seven of the top ten fish of the season were taken from stillwaters during the 1978/79 season — compared with seven out of ten the previous season and nine out of ten the season before that.

These stillwaters, often vast in area, also have the advantage of being largely ignored during the winter months by anglers other than the dedicated enthusiasts.

They offer the specimen hunter the best potential return for his efforts. Even though the existing pike record presents a massive target, the would-be record breaker can at least be certain of one thing — the stillwaters of this country offer the best chance of success.

Top pike, 1978/79:

33lb 8oz, Cambs pit, November 1978; Jim Carter, Wisbech, Cambs.
33lb, Private Kent lake, October 1978; Peter Richardson, Tunbridge Wells, Kent.
32lb, Ure, Boroughbridge, Yorks, October 1978; John Merrigan, Langley Park, Co. Durham.
31lb 12oz, Notts gravel pit, October 1978; Richard Siddall, Sheffield, Yorks.
31lb 8oz, Wye, Hay, Herefordshire, October 1978; Len Thomas, Trebanog, Glams.
31lb 2oz, Kennet, Kintbury, Wilts, January 1979; Reg Wiggins, Chiseldon, Wilts.
30lb 13oz, Hyde Lane Lake, Buckingham, June 1978; Mick Gunthorpe, Deanshanger, Bucks.
30lb 12oz, Cheshire reservoir, March 1979; Terry Knight, St Helens, Lancs.
30lb 8oz, Barham Pit, Ipswich, September 1978; George Lamb, Ipswich.
30lb 2oz, Hollowell reservoir, Northampton, January 1979; Geoff Smith, Northampton.

Mick Gunthorpe with one of the heaviest pike of the season. The fish scaled 30lb 13oz and was taken during the opening weeks of the season from a Buckingham lake.

Roach—simple tactics

The idea of pulling out a succession of small to medium-sized roach with quantity rather than quality in mind does not appeal to everyone.

But it's a fact that while most waters hold these fish, comparatively few hold 'specimens' — and in any case, the word 'specimen' should mean something significantly higher than the average size for a given water, not merely a fish that exceeds 2lb. So it often makes sense to accept your local water's limitations and aim to speed up your catch rate, while always hoping that the larger roach will come along.

The tactics to take a netful of roach vary depending on the type of water fished, but some things remain constant. The rod, for example. For floatfishing, a 12 or 13ft rod with a nice, fast tip action is ideal. The longer it is, the more control you will have when recovering line on the strike.

Reel line need never be more than 1.7lb, except when trotting a river with a heavy current . . . and this sort of fishing suggests you will be aiming at the larger roach, rather than the shoal fish. Hooks — the smaller, the better, down to perhaps size 22. If the roach still won't bite, a netful isn't on the cards however hard you try.

Let's look at two different situations when you may be expected to make a 'killing'. The first is a river in midsummer, where the level is down on normal but there is still a steady flow. The water is not gin clear, but neither is it heavily coloured, so the roach will be a little wary of clumsy tackle.

The river is subject to a fair amount of match pressure at weekends, but you are able to come midweek and select any swim you please.

This is a case where seed baits can often produce a 'fish a chuck' if you have the patience to work up the swim. Hemp is used to attract and preoccupy the roach, and then either more hemp or something resembling a superior version of it is introduced on the hook. Tares are a favourite.

The hemp should be boiled until it splits and the white kernel shows through. To put it on the hook, just push the bend into the split. Tares, which are also boiled before use, can be nicked under the skin.

Hook sizes for seed fishing can be larger than for maggots or casters. If you are using hemp on the hook, an 18 is about right, but for tares you can safely go up to a 14.

To get roach going on seeds, the first thing to remember is to feed little and often. Start with only a dozen grains of hemp catapulted or thrown into the head of the swim.

Follow this with the end tackle. Your float can be either a light waggler or a stick. The stick, attached both top and bottom, is the better choice because the progress of the bait can be checked without the float being submerged.

Shotting for hemp fishing sometimes poses problems as the roach go for the lead rather than the bait, though this does not happen as often as is thought. To overcome this, you can either use the special French 'mouse dropping' leads or bunch groups of No 8 (dust) shot evenly down the line.

Your first few trots down, each preceded by a few grains of loose hemp, will probably produce nothing. Then the float will reach almost the end of the swim and suddenly shoot down. Initial bites on hemp are very fast. Once the roach are in the swim, you can draw them closer and closer to you, until they are feeding almost under the rod tip.

But in order not to 'spook' the shoal, play each fish with caution. Keep the rod tip low, and try not to let hooked roach splash on the surface. On a 1.7lb line you can swing in anything under 6oz safely, but if in doubt use the net rather than risk a lost fish causing a disturbance.

There are two variations on hemp fishing. One, popular on the Thames, is to use an elderberry on the hook. The other is to feed something in with the loose hemp, in clear conditions, to colour up the water. One recipe consists of ground hemp mixed with molasses cattle feed.

There are two main reasons why roach can suddenly go off when using seed baits. The first is overfeeding, and the remedy is obvious. The second is that as the roach come up the swim, they also rise higher in the water to intercept the falling grains. Try shallowing up the distance between hook and float.

Our second situation is on a small reservoir in autumn. There are shallows at one end, and the depth increases to just over 13 feet at the dam end. The margins all round are quite shallow, but shelve very quickly to the full depth within a couple of rod lengths.

A general rule on stillwaters is to fish into the wind, so despite the discomfort, choose a swim that fulfils that condition. That same wind has disturbed silt on the bottom and that, together with an algal growth, has coloured the water. The roach will be feeding close on small items of food blown into the margins, so there is no point in trying to fish at distance. The wind will make conventional float tackle hard to control.

You can use a running line, but in these circumstances, a pole is so much more practical. Your aim is speed, remember, and it's no accident

A superb 50lb bag of roach which includes several specimens topping the 2lb mark. The fish came from a Midland stillwater.

that in Ireland, all the important international matches on the River Bann have been won with the pole.

The end tackle is simple — a crook at the end of the pole supporting your elastic, a tiny swivel between elastic and the main line, then your pole float, hook length (ready shotted and kept in readiness on a winder) and hook, which is a fine wire, size 18 or 20 caster type.

Swing out your float gently, keeping your range within the marginal shelf, so that the bait just brushes bottom. That bait is caster. Don't just shove the hook through it and expect to catch. Introduce the point into the top of the caster and then gently tap it in and round until the whole hook is completely buried. That's why caster hooks are of such fine wire, to prevent the bait being burst.

In coloured water, cereal groundbait is of little use. Just catapult in some loose feed around the float.

Some pole floats have really fine tips made of bristle, designed to register the most sensitive of bites. Those with a thicker tip are better. You can see them without eye strain, and in choppy conditions they are less prone to signalling false bites as the bait drags bottom and the wind takes the tip under. With this style of roaching, it is better to miss a few tentative bites and hook the more confident ones, rather than strike at everything and only prick your fish.

On stillwaters, a moving bait can often be deadly. Roach will take 'on the drop' as the bait is settling, or you can duplicate the effect by raising the rod tip every few seconds.

When using fine tackle in pursuit of a netful of roach, heavier fish — either roach, bream or chub — often turn up as a bonus. It's surprising how even a 1lb hook length can cope if there are no snags in the swim. As an experiment, tie a piece of your 1.7lb reel line to the tip ring of your rod, attach the other end to the crook of a spring balance and see if you can pull the breaking strain. You'll either fail or be amazed at the amount of pressure needed to do it.

A delighted angler with a 150lb catch from the River Sillees, Northern Ireland.

Top roach, 1978/79:

3lb 10oz, River Beult, Hunton, Kent, March 1979; Roger Sedge, Maidstone, Kent.
3lb 8oz, Bristol Avon, Somerford, November 1978; Thomas Rosse, Bristol.
3lb 5oz, Broxholme Lake, Selby, Yorks, September 1978; Vincent Greaves, Selby, Yorks.
3lb 4oz, River Welland, Tinwell, Lincs, March 1979; Philip Stubley, Stamford, Lincs.
3lb 4oz, Berkshire gravel pit, September 1978; Ashley Smith, Camberley, Surrey.
3lb 2oz, Leeds/Liverpool canal, November 1978; Ashley Hobson, Blackburn, Lancs.
3lb 1oz, Newton Pit, near Rugby, September 1978; Kevin Johnson, Rugby.
3lb 1oz, Forth and Clyde Canal, January 1979; Douglas Wallace, Alandale.
3lb, Kentish Stour, Canterbury, October 1978; Peter Ottewill, Croydon, Surrey.
3lb, Hampshire Avon, September 1978; Alan Bourne, Christchurch, Dorset.
3lb, Middle Hampshire Avon, October 1978; Neil Hurren, Bournemouth, Hants.
3lb, River Wensum, Fakenham, July 1978; Martin Parsons, Fakenham.
3lb, Thames, Oxford, August 1978; John Cadd, Oxford.

Perch

The 1978/79 season will surely be recorded as the season in which the existing perch record of 4lb 12oz came within a hairsbreadth of being broken. Each season sees a handful of reported fish above the record. But most of these superb specimens are usually returned to the water before they can be accurately witnessed or weighed.

Last season was the exception when Fred Oatley of Bath, Somerset, landed what he believed to be a new record fish. This time the fish was not only accurately weighed and witnessed, it was also photographed. Unfortunately for Fred the specimen tipped the scales at 4lb 11½oz, just ½oz beneath the record.

But Fred's capture does prove that the perch record is vulnerable and that there are plenty of waters, albeit lakes, ponds and gravel pits, which are capable of producing a new record breaker.

Fred took his fish from a private lake at Bath, a water quite clearly capable of producing even larger fish. The second largest fish of the season tipped the scales at 4lb 11oz and was taken from a private pool at Wombourne, Staffs.

Only three other fish over the 4lb mark were recorded — hardly surprising considering that few anglers now fish specifically for perch. The only other significant capture was a 4lb 5oz fish from the Key Transport Pond at Newton Abbot, Devon. This same water produced a 4lb 7oz fish the previous season and has obvious record potential.

The perch has long been one of the most attractive of the coarse fish species, both visually and as a quarry. Its bold, colourful, and distinctive markings are matched by its willingness to grab any bait that comes its way — especially as far as the smaller fish are concerned.

Sadly, stocks of perch were decimated by a mystery disease in the Sixties and, even now, the species is facing an uphill struggle to re-establish itself.

The perch fills a vital part in the ecological chain of our coarse fisheries. Its predatory, and scavenging, nature helps clear our waters of weak and sickly fish. Its comeback since that mystery disease has been made even more difficult by the introduction, both planned and illegal, of an alien species, the zander, into many top fisheries.

While the perch, which is essentially a shoal fish, can co-exist quite happily with that other main predator, the pike, a solitary fish, the introduction of the zander, a species which hunts in packs, has made its comeback even more difficult. There are few coarse anglers who can put their hands on their hearts and honestly maintain that they would rather catch specimen zander than specimen perch.

The perch has also, for many years, filled an important niche in the apprenticeship of the coarse angler. Small perch are, by nature, bold biters, prepared to attack most baits in a decisive, aggressive fashion.

Faced with a mealtime prospect of a juicy worm they will attack and refuse to let go until they have swallowed their meal. To the expert anglers these small fish are nothing but a nuisance. But to the novice or youngster they can be relied upon to provide exciting sport under conditions of extreme heat or cold when most other species refuse to feed.

Their fighting qualities should not be ignored either. Provided tackle is suitably scaled down they can be relied upon to give a good account of themselves.

The only bright spot on the horizon is the increasing number of these small fish which are beginning to turn up in many of our major rivers. Stillwater perch seemed to suffer less from the ravages of disease, although their numbers were significantly reduced. It was the river perch which were the hardest hit.

Their resurgence has been a long, slow, process and it is still uncertain whether they will ever re-establish themselves to their former density. The signs are certainly promising but by no means conclusive.

It remains a sad fact that on many of our top perch waters, those reservoirs reserved exclusively for trout fishing, the species is regarded as vermin. It seems madness that this fine sporting fish should be revered by one section of anglers, yet thrown up the bank in disgust by another. It is a sad reflection of the divisions which continue to affect our sport.

Top perch, 1978/79:

4lb 11½oz, private lake, Bath, Somerset, November 1978; Fred Oatley, Bath.
4lb 11oz, private pool, Wombourne, Staffs, August 1978; Peter Attley, Tipton, Staffs.
4lb 5oz, Pond, Newton Abbot, Devon, October 1978; Alan Preston, Newton Abbot.
4lb 2oz, Essex lake, December 1978; John Green, Waltham Abbey, Herts.
4lb 1½oz, Private Kent lake, January 1979; Alan Maxey, London.
3lb 15oz, Derwent, Yorks, July 1978; Trevor Spencer, Wheelgate Morton, Yorks.

Somerset angler Fred Oatley with the largest perch of the season. Fred's fish weighed 4lb 11½oz, just half an ounce under the existing British record.

Eel—how large do they

The capture of a new British Record eel of 11lb 2oz, in July 1978, finally proved that double-figure fish are a reality. And some would say it also opened the door to bigger and better eels becoming a regular feature of the angling scene.

This assumption does not stand up to scrutiny. For the eleven-pounder was so much heavier than anything caught before, and taken in such unusual circumstances, that it must be looked at quite apart from the general run of large eels.

The fish fell to a young Chichester angler, Stephen Terry, while he was carp fishing at Kingfisher Lake, in Hampshire. Despite its awesome size it was quite quickly beaten, photographed with the captor on the bank, and then taken home by Stephen. It died a few days later.

Bearing in mind the almost impossible brute strength of which a healthy fish even half that size is capable, it seems likely that the record-breaker was well over the hill. And the reason can be put down, not to any specific disease, but to old age. This would account for it being hooked during the day — unusual for a big eel — and for its poor performance. It was an atypical fish because it was an ancient fish.

Eels are among the longest-lived and most slow growing of freshwater dwelling species. A two-

Stephen Terry with his record 11lb 2oz eel. The exception that proves the rule?

Top eels, 1978/79:

8lb 3oz, Earlswood Lakes, Warwicks, August 1978; John Sidley, Birmingham.
7lb, River Rother, Kent, May 1978; Dale Mackett, Romney Marsh, Kent.
5lb 13oz, Northampton lake, April 1979; Mark Lister, Quorn, Leics.
5lb 6oz, Hertfordshire lake, November 1978; John Collins, Enfield, Middlesex.

grow?

pounder can be as much as 20 years old, by which time it will be sexually mature and ready to make its spawning run to the Sargasso Sea.

But of course, if all eels conformed to this pattern, four-pounders would be unheard of, and double-figure fish an impossibility. A look at the life cycle of the eel, and the way certain individuals deviate from the norm, will clear up the mystery.

The eel begins life about 70 fathoms down in the Sargasso, a breeding ground off the south coast of Bermuda in the Western Atlantic. Once the floating eggs are laid, the parent fish are assumed to die. The hatched young are leaf-shaped and called Leptocephali, a Latin name meaning leaf-shaped, which describes them perfectly.

The tiny fish gradually move across the Atlantic in an easterly direction, and by the time they are two years old they are approaching the coasts of Europe. Before they make the run up our rivers as elvers they change shape, becoming the familiar semi-transparent mini eels by the age of three.

Once into our waters, they move upstream, some taking up residence in the rivers themselves, others running up the tributaries or even crossing dry land at night during a heavy dew to come to rest in landlocked ponds, lakes and reservoirs. Here they will remain until the urge to breed drives them back down the rivers to make the journey to the Sargasso. The cycle is complete.

As an eel's migratory trip becomes imminent, the fish undergoes certain bodily changes. Its snout becomes sharper, its eyes larger and its general colour more silvery — in fact these fish are known as silver eels.

Not all eels make the journey as a matter of course. Certain individuals, which some authorities consider to be sterile females, remain in British waters where, over many years, they attain truly immense proportions.

It is interesting to note that Kingfisher Lake, where the eleven-pounder was taken, conforms exactly to the specifications laid down for a record-producing water by Birmingham eel expert John Sidley. John says that for a stillwater to be in with a chance of coming up with a record fish, it must have remained undrained for many years, and contained a steady supply of food for the growing eel. With a record of roach to over 3lb, Kingfisher Lake is not a water of stunted stock, nor is it a recently man-made fishery.

The muscle power of big eels, which can swim just as well backwards as they can forwards, means that accidental captures on conventional coarse tackle geared to other species are comparatively rare. Many eels are hooked, of course, only to snap the line. Pike anglers fishing deadbaits pick up their share, but in general the capture of big eels is a deliberate, not an accidental affair.

And while eels aren't everyone's cup of tea, there is an increasing number of specimen hunters who concentrate on nothing else. The eleven-pounder will have spurred them to greater things, but what are their chances of success?

To begin with, these cannot be forecast on the basis of captures over the last decade or so. With roach or bream, a bad spawning can show its effects in very few years, and with factors like disease, one can predictably and accurately trace future population size. With eels we are working on a much longer time scale. The present record, for example, could have swum up our rivers as an elver well before the outbreak of World War One.

There are no signs as yet that the run of elvers has decreased significantly, despite heavy netting in places like the Severn estuary. And even if the elvers were being over-exploited, this would not begin to have a traceable effect on adult eels for many years to come.

There is no such thing, either, as a 'good' or a 'bad' eel year. The number of fish reported over 5lb is so small each season that the variation can be attributed to chance.

Of more significance is the 'fashion' for particular eel waters. In the late sixties, for example, the Grand Union Canal near Northampton was the centre of much attention and anglers including Bob Church, now better known for his trouting, took many fish over 5lb. The best was a 6¼-pounder by Essex angler Peter Bunce in June 1968.

Now the Grand Union is out of favour, and the most concerted efforts to crack the record are being made in the Birmingham area by members of the 'Put Eels Back' campaign, headed by John Sidley. John's best fish to date is an 8lb 3oz specimen from Earlswood Lake, but he has hooked and lost an eel which he estimated by comparison to be in low double figures. So the potential is there.

To locate a water holding very large eels is only half the battle. These fish lie up in swims which are almost invariably snag-ridden, which increases the already obvious need for heavy tackle. Just what the fight of a healthy double-figure fish is like cannot be judged on the evidence of one angler's experience.

What is certain, however, is that eels far in excess of the present British Record are there for the taking. But they present such an awesome challenge that it is doubtful if one will ever be put on the bank by fair angling.

Carp — recipe for success

It is ironic that one branch of angling, the pursuit of big carp, has become almost as much of a rat race as the pressurised existence from which the hobby is supposed to be an escape.

Never before have so many anglers turned their attention to carp, and never before has carping been so competitive. At times it seems the carp man is pitting his wits, not only against the fish, but against every other angler on the bank.

It is perhaps time to step aside for a moment, and reflect that the British record fish of 44lb was caught on the simplest of baits . . . bread. And even today, four of the ten heaviest carp reported to Angling Times in the 1978/79 season fell to that most reliable standby from the baker's shop.

Clearly, then, for all the scientific advances in carp baits, there is still a case for simplicity of approach.

A Thames carp double — fish of 23lb 1oz and 15lb 7oz, taken from the river at Kingston.

The aforementioned bread is still top of the league. Even users of real exotica admit that if they were restricted to one bait,that would be it.

Bread can be used torn straight from a new loaf, in flake form. The crust can be cut off and used as a deadly floating bait. Or it can be combined with bread paste to form 'balanced crust' which sinks really slowly and is invaluable when the lake bottom is composed of soft weed or mud.

Paste itself can either be used plain, or mixed with any additive that takes your fancy, and preferably that of the carp, too. Honey is an old favourite. Try custard powder paste, or that milk shake powder that comes in a variety of fruit flavours. Among savoury pastes, those made with sardines or pilchards are quite popular.

Potatoes have always been quoted as a good carp bait, but they most definitely don't work on every water and something better can nearly always be found. To be effective, they must be boiled soft, not parboiled.

Cat and dog food, mixed with cereal as a stiffener, can be a great carp killer, and sausage meat kneaded into a stiff paste with breadcrumbs is worth a look. To this basic paste mixture can be added almost anything which the angler thinks will increase his chances. We are now moving into the realm of the 'special'.

Broadly a 'special' bait is something mixed to the angler's own recipe, which can't be bought ready made up over the counter. The fashion now is to buy ingredients which are commonly acknowledged to be good carp takers, but combine them in one's own proportions. Many of these specialist ingredients are high in protein, and quite expensive.

A couple of seasons back, the aim was to achieve the highest possible protein content in 'special' baits, even though no less an authority than the record-holder, Dick Walker, pointed out that no fish could analyse the food value of a bait.

Now, it is acknowledged that to be effective, a carp bait must fulfil other qualities. First, it must be attractive — taste and smell good. Second, it must not frighten the fish, and the best way to ensure this is to vary not only its composition, but also its shape and presentation.

With 'special' baits, it is policy to throw a few sample balls into the chosen swim and follow it up with the baited hook. Another category which encompasses a wide range of choice, is mass and particle baits. For this style of fishing, the 'free offerings' or mass form a carpet on the bed of the swim, and the baited hook is picked up as the fish vacuums over that carpet.

Particle baits include sweetcorn, peas, broad beans, raisins, maggots and a variety of dried beans and peas which can be bought from delicatessens. These should always be boiled before being introduced into the swim, or they will swell inside the carps' stomachs and kill them.

Among live baits, worms — including lobs, redworms and brandlings — are worth considering. So are mealworms, which are really beetle larvae. But perhaps the best meat bait comes out of a tin . . . luncheon meat.

Trout pellet paste has gone out of favour a little since the makers changed the recipe. But you can still buy trout or salmon crumbs, distinguishable by their strong fish smell. They can simply be mixed with boiling water and kneaded to a consistency that will stay on the hook.

The most modern baits in the carp angler's armoury have been developed in the laboratory, rather than the kitchen. Before using them, you should find out whether the carp on your local water have encountered them before. If they have, you will need less of this bait, which is quite pricey, in order to interest the fish.

These baits, which are marketed under a proprietary name, contain a number of pure chemicals including amino acids, that act as attractors to foraging carp. They can either be fished over free samples, or in conjunction with a separate attractor ingredient which is mixed with a fast break-up meal.

Top carp, 1978/79:

35lb 4oz, Healey Dam, Ossett, Yorks, September 1978; Anthony Emmitt, Wakefield, Yorks.
33lb 2oz, Ashlea Pool, Gloucs, September 1978; Kevin Maddocks, Enfield, Middlesex.
32lb, Southampton club water, September 1978; Chris Currie, Fairoak, Hants.
32lb, Royal Military Canal, Ashford, Kent, October 1978; Bill Phillips, Ashford.
31lb 8oz, Mid Northants carp fishery, Higham Ferrers, November 1978; Roger Holton, Higham Ferrers.
30lb 1oz, Darenth lake, Kent, November 1978; James Chitty, Swanley, Kent.
29lb 4oz, Tri-Lakes, Surrey, September 1978; Bill Linkson, London.
26lb 2oz, private pit, Bucks, August 1978; Ian Herrington, Chalfont, Bucks.
24lb 15oz, Brooklands Lake, Kent, August 1978; Gary Vincent, Dartford, Kent.
24lb 12oz, Medway, Yalding, October 1978; Stephen Robbins, Maidstone, Kent.

Chub

The chub record of 7lb 6oz must surely be one of the most vulnerable records on the coarse fish list. There are plenty of waters capable of producing a specimen far in excess of that weight.

Yet each season the record remains intact, proving that either the chub enthusiast is not as competent as other specimen hunters or that big chub are far harder to catch than appearances would suggest.

In fairness to the angler it is now quite clear that big chub are among the most difficult to lure. Izaak Walton called them the 'most fearfullest of fishes' hundreds of years ago and that great angler wasn't far wrong in his assessment of various species.

The chub is essentially a shoal fish and the largest of them all are the canniest survivors of an original shoal. The fact that they have outlived all their brothers and sisters is a testimony to their cunning and certainly doesn't make the angler's task any easier.

Really big chub also have the annoying habit of taking up residence in the most inaccessible swims on the river.

They often lie right under the banks, in a tangle of roots and branches, inspecting each morsel of food brought down by the current, with the utmost caution. Tempting them with a bait, which often has to be presented in the most natural form possible on the smallest of hooks and lightest of lines, is difficult enough.

Having hooked them the angler is then faced with the added problem of bullying them from the safety of their lair on tackle which is usually not strong enough to withstand their first surging run.

It's fair to say that more specimen chub are hooked and lost then any other coarse fish species. And pricked fish have a habit of learning from their mistakes, becoming progressively harder to deceive.

The one chink in the specimen chub's armour is its aggressiveness, especially during the early part of the season. A great many record-breaking chub have been landed by fly fishermen — who have either tossed the fish up the bank in disgust or thrown them back into the water simply because they lacked the spots, and gullibility of those anglers quarry, the trout.

Fly fishing — a method rarely used by the specimen hunter — has a double advantage. The

The chub, willing to feed under most conditions, is becoming an increasingly popular quarry.

fly can be floated down to the most inaccessible of spots — areas favoured by really big chub. And the largest chub can be stalked and provoked into taking if a fly is dropped, with a splash, right on their tails.

A surprising number of big fish have fallen to this method. It's as if the natural aggression of the fish forces it to take the bait instinctively.

But for the majority of anglers the importance of the chub lies not in the size of the fish, but in its willingness to accept a wide variety of baits under a variety of different conditions. The fish has a large mouth in proportion to its body size and a voracious appetite to match.

It will feed during the hottest days of summer and the coldest days of winter. And it can usually be relied upon to give a good account of itself if the angler is prepared to scale his tackle down accordingly.

Chub are essentially a shoal fish and once one has been landed it's a fair bet that the angler will hook others too.

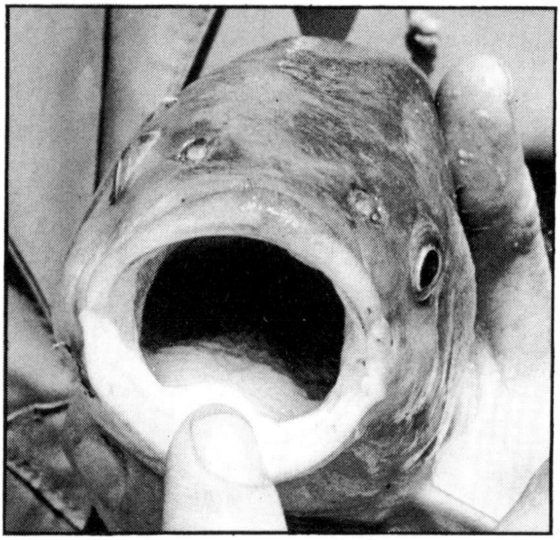

Chub have large mouths — and appetites to match. They can be caught on a variety of baits.

Big bags of chub can be landed, under the right conditions, by relatively inexperienced anglers giving the novice some compensation for all those frustrating outings during the season when he catches little or nothing.

The best chub fishing is traditionally in autumn and winter and the season's results were adversely affected by the weather. The constant floods which swept the major chub rivers did more harm than the freezing weather.

Chub soon adapt to temperature change but quickly go off the feed on a rising river. But despite the weather big fish — and good catches of smaller fish — were taken. True only one seven pounder, a fish from the Suffolk Stour, was recorded. But six pounders were taken from at least seven different rivers, ranging from the Ribble to the Kentish Eden.

A six pound chub is a true specimen by any standard and it is fair to say that more rivers are capable of turning up a specimen chub than of providing a 20lb pike or 8lb bream. The finest chub river in England, the Severn, doesn't even figure in the season's top ten list!

And if the Severn has untapped chub potential so too has the River Trent, another water which also fails to make the list. In fairness both rivers provided more than their share of small and medium-sized fish during the season — and gave a great deal of pleasure to a great many anglers in the process.

But sorting out the larger fish, from the massive shoals, has proved a real problem to the serious specimen hunter. His task has not been helped by the sheer size of these rivers which makes stalking individual fish an impossiblity.

But even if the chub record stands for another twenty years there can be no denying the increasingly significant part played by the chub in catch returns. It has rapidly established itself as one of the mainstay species on our major rivers — and few anglers would complain about that.

Top chub, 1978/79:

7lb 2oz, Suffolk Stour, December 1978; Rod Wright, Sudbury.
6lb 14oz, Eden, Edenbridge, Kent, November 1978; Mike Andrews, Edenbridge.
6lb 13oz, Swale, Yorks, October 1978; Francis Collins, Rotherham, Yorks.
6lb 8oz, Hospital Lake, Staffs, July 1978; Alan Fryer, Stoke-on-Trent, Staffs.
6lb 5oz, Ribble, Balderstone, Lancs, March 1979; Ian Fairclough, Wigan.
6lb 4oz, Derwent, Yorks, September 1978; Rod Young, Hull.
6lb 4oz, Kennet, Newbury, Berks, July 1978; Paul Wakeley, Maidenhead.
6lb 3oz, Thames, Oxford, November 1978; Chris Timms, Oxford.
6lb 2oz, Lee Broxbourne, Herts, March 1979; James Wicks, Harlow, Essex.
6lb 2oz, Kennet, Reading, Berks, March 1979; Bob Buteux, London.

Tench—traditional ways

A bit of a revolution is taking place today in tench fishing, with new baits and new techniques scoring heavily on waters which have, in the past, yielded up their good tench rather sparingly.

At the same time traditional methods are also fishing well, so that it seems to me tench fishing itself is improving in quality. The new techniques, effective though they undoubtedly are, are really only partially responsible for the success seen in the last two or three years.

Added to this there is a new interest in tench fishing, partly, I suspect, because numbers of anglers have opted out of the highly competitive world of carp fishing. Leading the new thinking on tench is the Tenchfishers Club whose members employ both traditional and modern methods to capture their beloved quarry. Well, what are the well-tried old methods, and are they as good as the new approach?

In the first place one associated tench fishing with float fishing at relatively close range, say up to 25 yards, usually using a line of 4-6lb breaking strain and the smallest float needed for casting and/or visibility.

It doesn't much matter what the float is, as long as it carries enough shot to cast the bait, and shows enough tip above the water to make it visible. Again, traditionally, the float is attached at both ends, and the shot is mostly bunched about twelve inches from the hook and the depth set so that the shot just lies on the bottom: laying on, it is called. In the event of a bite the float may bob and sway a little, even lay flat, or perhaps slide away steadily out of sight.

As a matter of fact I have always parted with tradition here, even as a small boy preferring to attach the float at the bottom end only unless I wished to drag a bait slowly through the swim using wind drift.

Another traditional method of float fishing, and one which I am sure will never be replaced or improved upon, is the lift method. Here the shot, usually one swan shot, is placed only 1-2 inches from the hook. The depth is set almost exactly at the depth of the water, and the bite is indicated by the float riding high out of the water, the strike being made simultaneously. This would be using in the modern idiom, a particle bait: stewed wheat, puffed wheat, rice, caster, sweetcorn, or even the humble maggot.

A technique which is often an improvement on both the above methods is the float leger. In this case a single shot is used to stop a small Arlesey Bomb, at a variable distance from the bait. The tackle is set over depth and the rod placed in rests. Then the line is slowly tightened so that the float cocks. Bites using this method are usually very positive indeed, and the method has the advantage that distance is no problem.

All these methods work extremely well, and I have had good catches using them. I think in the past quite long rods were used for tench fishing, but round about the 1950s rods of about 10 feet came into use, such as the Mark IV Avon.

But, on swims with a wide marginal rush growth, there is terrific advantage in using a long rod. Today the rod can be a 14 foot hollow glass match rod. Using such a rod only recently I had tench of 4lb 10oz, 4lb 12oz and 5lb 7oz. In each case the long rod helped greatly to push the fish away from the margins, before they tired a little and were ready to be netted.

On that trip I had a float carrying 3 BB shot attached at both ends, and was laying on six inches in nine feet of water: a thoroughly traditional technique, except that I used a modern glass rod and sweetcorn bait, currently the 'in' bait.

I've given a hint above of what are the modern methods. Firstly legering, which arose from the world of big fish hunting in the 1950s and later spread to the match fishing world. Famous anglers such as Frank Guttfield made as valuable a contribution in this sphere as did the Taylor brothers with the lift method.

Legering can be deadly, although perhaps less enjoyable than watching a float at close range. But since the 1960s yet more innovations have taken place such as the extensive use of swing tips (excellent except when using big lob baits) and swim feeders.

The last is probably the most important modern tenching technique, and no serious tench fisherman can be without his swim feeders in various shapes and sizes. Coupled with standard link-leger techniques these methods enable the angler to fish at long range in swims previously untouched by traditional float methods.

Lastly there is the question of baits. Traditionally it is lobworm, brandling, flake and, more recently, maggots. Today it is sweetcorn, sweetcorn, and yet more sweetcorn! To be serious though particle baits have produced terrific tench catches in modern times and coupled with swim feeders and long range legering may be regarded as the pinnacle of modern technique and modern bait.

Similarly traditional baits and modern legering also succeed well. It seems to me that the man prepared to master both close range float work and long range leger work will have the best of both worlds. I don't think the one is better than the other.

are best? by Barrie Rickards

A catch of tench from a heavily-fished public water. The fish were taken on legered bread during an early-morning session during the opening week of the season.

Top tench, 1978/79:

9lb 11oz, Frimley Pit, Surrey, July 1978; Ron Seal, Farnborough, Hants.
9lb 6oz, Lake at Harefield, Middlesex, July 1978; Peter Lambert, South Harrow.
8lb 11oz, Private Surrey lake, July 1978; Fred Jenkins, Broadstairs, Kent.
8lb 6½oz, Club lake, Hants, July 1978; Phil Smith, Coventry.
8lb 4oz, Papercourt Pit, Surrey, August 1978; Philip Chudley, Guildford, Surrey.
8lb 1oz, Staffs mere, July 1978; Peter Cleaver, Stafford.
7lb 14oz, Oxfordshire lake, August 1978; Graham Baldwin, Oxford.
7lb 12oz, Harefield Pits, Middlesex, July 1978; Mike Voller, Watford, Herts.
7lb 12oz, Oxfordshire lake, July 1978; Tony Willis, Oxford.
7lb 10oz, Oxfordshire lake, July 1978; Tony Willis, Oxford.
7lb 10oz, Harefield Pits, Middlesex, July 1978; Mike Voller, Watford, Herts.

Barbel

The 1978/79 barbel season was certainly no record-breaker but it was, at least, the season during which the Hampshire Avon, the most celebrated barbel river in England, bounced right back into the reckoning.

Barbel are traditionally a fish of summer and autumn, losing their massive appetites and lapsing into a state of semi-hibernation once the water temperatures cool and autumn turns to winter. With the 1978/79 season consisting of a mediocre summer, a slightly above average autumn and an almost unfishable winter, the barbel was perhaps the least affected of all the coarse fish species.

This huge Kennet barbel was the fifth heaviest of the season. Captor Barry Bendall took it from a swim at the bottom of his garden.

Not surprisingly results, in terms of the weights of the top ten fish, were almost the same as the previous season, the only difference being the venues from which the best fish were taken.

It was here that the Hampshire Avon once again sprang to pre-eminence. No fewer than seven of the top ten fish were taken from the river, in sharp contrast to figures of one and three in the previous two seasons.

Burgate was the top venue on the river, accounting for five of those seven fish as well as a handful of slightly lesser double-figure fish. Even the Royalty fishery, once the most prolific stretch in terms of double-figure fish, enjoyed a sudden upsurge both in popularity and quality of fish.

Although it failed to figure in the top ten list, partly because of the tremendous pressure on the water which militates against the success of the serious specimen hunter, it nevertheless yielded its best returns for a number of seasons with dozens of fish in the 6-9lb class.

Specimen barbel are as difficult to catch as specimens of any other species, and while there are undoubtedly plenty of double-figure specimens present in the Royalty stretch conditions are hardly conducive to their capture by serious specimen hunters.

Peak time for catches of specimen barbel is undoubtedly the early autumn months. Not surprisingly eight of the top ten fish were taken during September, October and November, a period made even more fertile than usual by a prolonged spell of mild weather during those first two months.

The largest barbel of the year, a 12lb 10oz fish, came from the Kennet during August. Although the Kennet produces fewer specimen fish than the Avon, it can usually be relied upon to produce the

Top barbel, 1978/79:

12lb 10oz, Kennet, Berks, August 1978; Peter Cranstoun, Tadley, Hants.
12lb 4oz, Hants Avon, Burgate, October 1978; Albert Godfrey, London.
12lb, Hants Avon, Burgate, October 1978; Ray Borras, Barton-le-Clay, Beds.
11lb 8oz, Hants Avon, Ringwood, November 1978; Derek Turton, Hillingdon, Middlesex.
11lb 6oz, Kennet, Reading, November 1978; Barry Bendall, Reading.
11lb 6oz, Great Ouse, Offord, August 1978; Roger Baker, Oakley, Beds.
11lb 4oz, Hants Avon, Burgate, November 1978; Geoff Scott, Harlow, Essex.
11lb 4oz, Hants Avon, Burgate, November 1978; David Furness, Maidenhead, Berks.
11lb 2oz, Hants Avon, Ringwood, September 1978; Paul Sheppard, Basingstoke, Hants.
10lb 14oz, Hants Avon, October 1978; Bill Privett, Romford, Essex.

odd really large specimen, usually a 12 pounder.

Its most popular stretches are subject to far less angling pressure than the Hampshire Avon and it must surely offer a very real chance of success to the would-be record breaker. As well as supplying the best fish of the year it also provided an 11lb 6oz specimen in November.

The two other 12 pounders taken during the season both came from the Avon at Burgate during October. The only other water to figure in the top ten list was the Great Ouse, a traditional supplier of odd, extremely large specimens.

The best Ouse fish tipped the scales at 11lb 6oz and was taken at Offord by specimen hunter Roger Baker in August. Ouse barbel may be relatively few and far between but when caught are invariably large.

They are confined to relatively few areas of the river and certainly grow large enough to threaten the existing British record of 13lb 12oz.

The most prolific barbel river is, of course, the Severn. Large stretches of the middle river of this mighty water are alive with shoals of small barbel offering hectic sport for the pleasure angler. Once again several 'ton-up' pleasure catches of the smaller fish were recorded with plenty of 5, 6 and 7lb fish being recorded too.

The barbel population of the river now seems to be stabilising after the population explosion of the early Seventies.

Significantly, at least for the specimen hunter, this means that there is now more chance of taking a double-figure specimen. In previous seasons the vast mass of barbel in the river has made it difficult for the angler to sort out the better quality fish.

Until the start of the last season only seven double-figure fish had been recorded from the river — a derisory figure in comparison with the number of barbel landed. The 1978/79 was no record breaker but it did at least produce two Severn fish of 10½lb.

The barbel potential of the river is completely untapped and if the population has now peaked, and is more likely to decline than increase, the chances of the river producing a record breaker may well encourage more anglers to concentrate on those really big fish.

This fine catch of barbel was taken from the River Severn at Atcham during a match. Captor Brian Warren weighed in 68lb with individual fish to 5½lb. Severn barbel stocks are now levelling off and chances of specimen fish increase each season.

Record Fish

Clarissa, the record carp. Dick Walker has held the record with this 44lb fish since 1952.

Barbel	13	12	0	1962	J. Day, Royalty Fishery, Hants.
Bleak	0	3	15	1971	D. Pollard, Staythorpe Pond, Nr. Newark, Notts.
Bream	13	8	0	1977	A. R. Heslop, private water, Staffs.
Bullhead	0	0	10	1978	E. Harrison, Leeds & Liverpool Canal, Leach Bridge.
Carp	44	0	0	1952	R. Walker, Redmire Pool.
Carp, Crucian	5	10	8	1976	G. Halls, at lakes Nr. King's Lynn, Norfolk.
Catfish	43	8	0	1970	R. J. Bray, Wilstone Reservoir, Tring, Herts.
Char	1	12	4	1974	C. Imperiale, Loch Insh, Inverness-shire.
Chub	7	6	0	1957	W. L. Warren, Royalty Fishery, Hants.
Dace	1	4	4	1960	J. L. Gasson, Little Ouse, Thetford, Norfolk.
Eel	11	2	0	1978	S. Terry, Kingfisher Lake, Nr. Ringwood, Hants.
Gudgeon	0	4	4	1977	M. J. Bowen, Fish Pond, Ebbw Vale, Gwent, Wales.
Gwyniad	1	4	0	1965	J. R. Williams, Llyn Tegid, Wales.
Loch Lomond Powan	1	7	0	1972	J. M. Ryder, Loch Lomond, Scotland.
Minnow	0	0	9	1978	R. Guy, River Rother, Nr. Midhurst, Sussex.
Golden Orfe	4	3	0	1976	B. T. Mills, River Test, Hampshire.
Perch	4	12	0	1962	S. F. Baker, Oulton Broad, Suffolk.
Pike	40	0	0	1967	P. D. Hancock, Horsey Mere, Norfolk.
Pike-Perch (Walleye)	11	12	0	1934	F. Adams, The Delph, Welney, Norfolk.
Pike-Perch (Zander)	17	4	0	1977	D. Litton, Great Ouse Relief Channel.
Pumpkinseed	0	2	10	1977	A. Baverstock, G.L.C. Highgate Pond, London.
Roach	4	1	0	1975	R. G. Jones, Notts Gravel Pit.
Rudd	4	8	0	1933	Rev. E. C. Alston, Thetford, Norfolk.
Ruffe	0	5	0	1977	P. Barrowcliffe, River Bure, St. Benets Abbey, Norfolk.
Salmon	64	0	0	1922	Miss G. W. Ballantyne, River Tay, Scotland.
Schelly	1	10	0	1976	W. Wainwright, Ullswater, Cumbria.
Tench	10	1	2	1975	L. W. Brown, Peterborough, Brick Pit.
Trout American Brook	4	8	8	1978	A. Pearson, Avington Fishery, Hampshire.
Trout Brown	19	9	4	1978	J. A. F. Jackson, Loch Quoich, Inverness-shire, Scotland.
Trout Rainbow	19	8	0	1977	A. Pearson, Avington Fishery, Hampshire.

Species open for claims: grayling, minimum qualifying weight 3lb; sea trout, 20lb; silver bream, 1 lb 8oz.

INSPIRED CASTING!
Intrepid and Sealey, the ideal partnership of rod and reel.
Intrepid and Sealey make the most versatile team in fishing today. We have the right reels, rods and hooks as well as the right Gladding lines and leaders. On stream, river or reservoir, the Intrepid Sealey combination has everything you need to make the day perfect.
We are unique in Britain, in making every type of tackle ourselves, Our service is famous and we experiment constantly with new ideas and developments. Give Intrepid Sealey your casting vote whether you are a fly, sea or coarse fisherman. We have a complete range of up-to-date and economic tackle for you.
Intrepid Sealey
The most versatile name in fishing
Intrepid Sealey Ltd.
Intrepid Works Falmouth,
Cornwall TR11 4RS
Tel: (0326) 72441

Match Fishing

by Peter Maskell

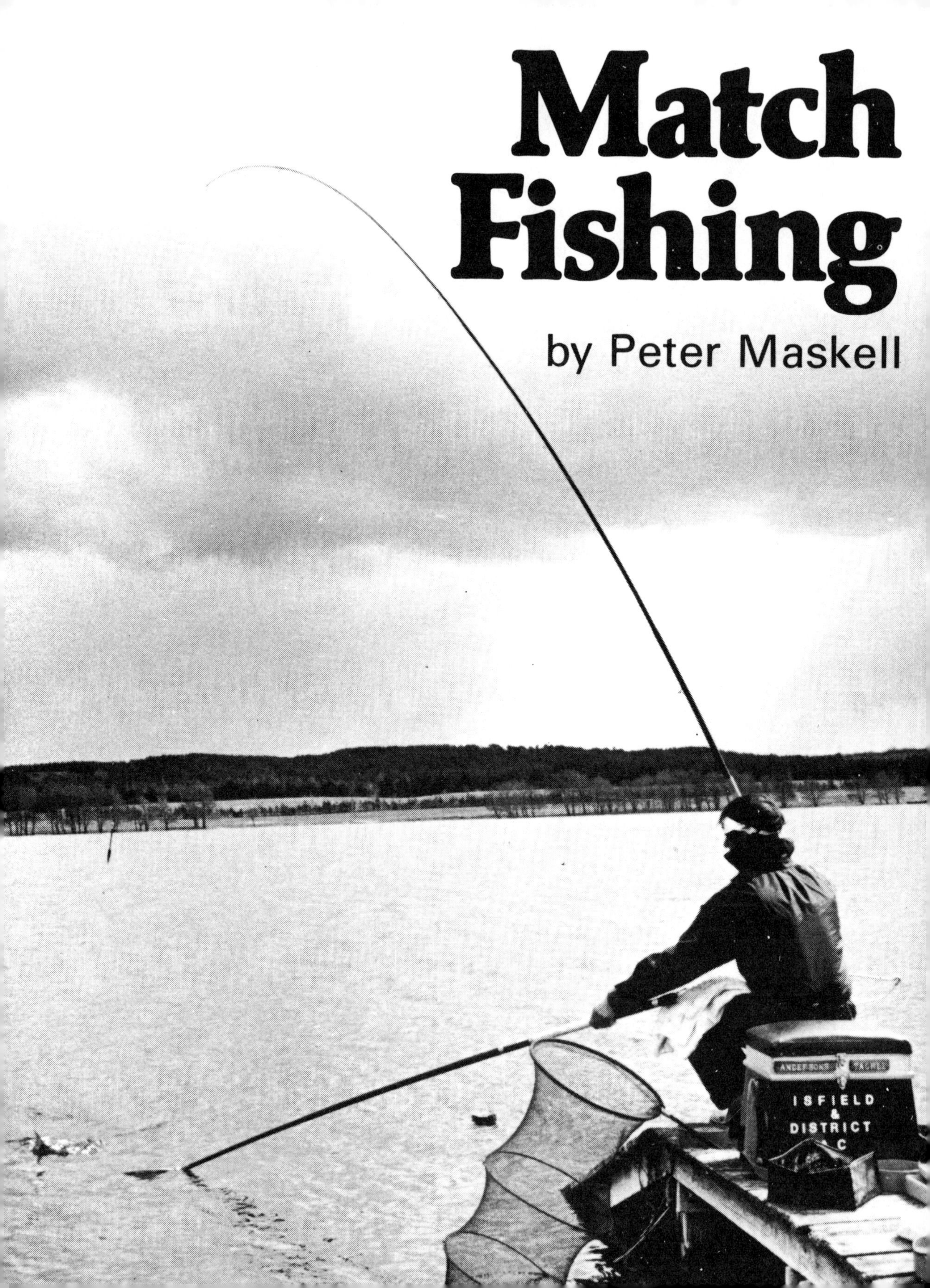

The last 12 months of the match angling scene have seen some radical changes in the open match circuit. Anglers, who a few years ago, thought nothing of a 2-300 mile round trip to fish a match, are now concentrating on their local circuit, waters within a few miles of their homes.

The reasons are self-evident. Match fishing has become, during the last few years, increasingly expensive, especially for the man who fishes two, or even three matches a week. The matchman has had during the last twelve months, to face soaring travelling costs caused by the rise in petrol prices. And if that's not a large enough extra burden he has also been faced with, in certain areas, a shortage of fuel.

The end result has been to limit the distance that anglers, who wish to compete on the open match circuit, are now prepared to travel. Most matchmen certainly don't fish for cash rewards, even the top men are lucky if they show a profit at the end of the season. But there comes a point where any man, no matter how much he enjoys his favourite pastime, must call a halt to the expenditure on his particular hobby.

Petrol prices, and availability, have been a crucial factor in the changing match scene. During the foreseeable future there will no longer be a single, accepted open match circuit. Instead there will be a number of open circuits growing up in each region of the country. Standards of match angling may be slightly downgraded but the potential benefits to local clubs will far outweigh this.

A strengthening of regional circuits is bound to lead to a strengthening of water-holding clubs in a particular area, both financially and in standards of skill. Club matches, and the occasional club opens, have become increasingly important.

Most clubs throughout the country are faced with ever-increasing rent demands for their waters, as well as the perennial problems of pollution and abstraction. Increased revenue will at least allow them to hold their own and, hopefully, extend the amount and quality of the fishing they have to offer.

The main events of the last 12 months have seen a whole new crop of records and outstanding performances. The world five-hour match catch record was comprehensively shattered when Dennis Willis weighed in 207lb 8oz in the Fermanagh festival on the Erne at Enniskillen. Irish match fishing potential still remains largely untapped, a fact that is of little consolation to English matchmen.

The English season had few high spots. Appalling weather conditions for much of the season kept weights low on the major English match rivers. Winning, in many areas, was simply a matter of drawing the right peg, with skill counting for nothing.

Even the Severn and Trent, normally among the most consistent of venues, suffered badly from the weather conditions. But at least the Trent did give the top angler a chance to show his skills and success could be judged in terms of application and angling ability.

The unpredictable nature of the major rivers was a direct cause of some amazing upsets in the major matches. In the three Angling times Winter League semi-finals, none of the hot favourites managed to qualify. Even the Final, fished on the River Blackwater in Ireland, produced a major upset when outsiders Isfield carried off the trophy in convincing style.

But it would be unfair to attribute every major upset to the poor form of the major waters. The standard of match angling levels off each year and the gap between the average match angler and the top matchman narrows each season. Outsiders are no longer no-hopers, but competent men, quite capable of taking their chances if Lady Luck smiles their way at the draw bag.

Every match season throws up a handful of heroes, men who finally attain the triumphs that have eluded them for years. So it was in the 1978/79 season when Bryan Lakey of Wisbech won the richest prize of all, the Embassy Challenge. Bryan, who won the 1970 National, is one of the best bream anglers in the country, as well as being a true gentleman of the open match circuit.

His second major victory was long overdue and proof that the nice guys aren't always destined to come second. His victory is a salutary lesson to all would-be top matchmen — the previous year he'd sat next to the Embassy runner-up and failed to break double-figures.

The same match produced yet another tremendous performance by the 1978 winner, Ivan Marks. Happy-go-lucky Ivan came within a single fish of being the only man to win the coveted title twice.

Yet even in defeat he could still manage the smile-and-a-joke that have become the trade mark of this brilliant angler.

The third hero was mighty Kevin Ashurst, the angler who has been written off so many times by the bankside pundits. Kevin topped the Money Winners table to end a lean spell of several seasons and few men on the circuit would begrudge him that success.

The Big Matches

1978-79 Season

Wreake Championships: A Harris, Thurmaston, 5lb 5oz.
Wye Championships: Maurice Dutfield, Worcester, 51lb.
Yorkshire Ouse Championships: Bill Tomlinson, Castleford, 23lb 12½oz.
LAA Thames Championships: Brian Adams, XL, 20lb 10oz. Team: Trev's Terrapins.

Nene champion, Allan Haines.

Nene Championships: Allan Haines, Peterborough, 10lb 2oz.
Norfolk Broads Championships: Nick Larkin, Suffolk, 17lb 10½oz.
Soar Championships: Roy Henson, East Leake, 16lb 7oz.
Warwickshire Avon Championships: Bob Bignell, Redditch, 26lb 10½oz.
Idle Championships: Andrew Hancock, Doncaster, 3lb 8½oz.
Waveney Championships: L Saunders, Harleston, 127lb 6oz.
Middle Ouse Championships: Ken Roberts, Coventry, 18lb 1½oz.
Staffs Canal Championships, Trent and Mersey Canal: Bob Sippitts, Stratford, 6lb 10oz.
Calder Championships: Roy Duckett, Goole, 11lb 10oz.
Coronation Channel Championships: Kim Headon. Swinton, 9lb 3oz.
Upper Thames Championships: Reg Cooke, Team Dells, 39lb 6½oz.
Ancholme Championships: Roy Drakes, Scunthorpe, 33lb 13½oz.
Wharfe Championships: Howard Robson, Leeds, 12lb 5oz.
Suffolk Stour Championships: Colin Davies, Billericay Jokers, 21lb 11oz.

Trent champion, John Toulson.

Trent Championships: John Toulson, Nottingham, 17lb 14oz.
Bristol Avon Championships: Mike Young, Trev's Terrapins, 20lb 9½oz.

Vinnie Walsh, Huntspill champion.

Huntspill Championships: Vinnie Walsh, Leigh, 41lb 14oz.
Sibsey Trader Championships: Tony Woods, Grimsby, 12lb 8oz.
South Holland Championships: Graham Eden, Mansfield, 15lb 11½oz.
Severn Championships: Ernie Tilley, Stourbridge, 35lb 7oz.
Arun Championships: Mick Miller, Steyning, 24lb 7oz.
Lincolnshire Championships, Witham: Lol Lax, Sheffield, 31lb 2½oz.
Weaver Championships: Bill Edwards, Nantwich, 18lb 12oz.
Welland Championships: Brian Thompson, Sheffield, 13lb 7½oz.

King's Sedgemoor Championships: Roger Ackers, Farnborough, 12lb 3oz.
Southern England Championships, River Lee: Dave Richardson, Swindon Talisman, 14lb 6½oz.
Fermanagh Championships: Jim Douglas, Belfast, 64lb 0½oz.
Welsh National Championships, River Dee: Richie Bainton, Cardiff Nomads, 9lb 1½oz.
Scottish National Championships, Forth and Clyde Canal: Ian Cass, Border Coarse, 4lb 1oz.
North of England Championships, River Wharfe: Howard Robson, Compton Arms, 18lb.
Lower Trent Anglers' Alliance Championships: Paul Cope, Nottingham, 13lb.
Essex Individual Championships, River Lee: Barry Clark, Defiant Mobile, 5lb 14½oz.
Grimsby ASA Championships, Witham: Brian Cartwright, Humber Graving Docks A, 29lb 8oz.
LAA Open Championships, Grand Union Canal: Ricky Himpsen, 9lb 4oz.
Batemans Brewery Championships, River Steeping: George Warren, Boston, 18lb 13oz.
Leeds ASA Championships, Yorkshire Ouse: Phil Wilson, Leeds, 42lb 13oz.
Foseeco Championships, River Welland: Terry Jackson, Rotherham, 15lb 7oz.
Steelworkers Championships, River Welland: John Hill, Leeds, 9lb 4½oz.
Bass North West Championships, Lancaster Canal: David Williams, Bolton, 6lb 9oz.
Greenall Whitley Championships, River Weaver: Ian Roberts, Warrington, 12lb 15oz.

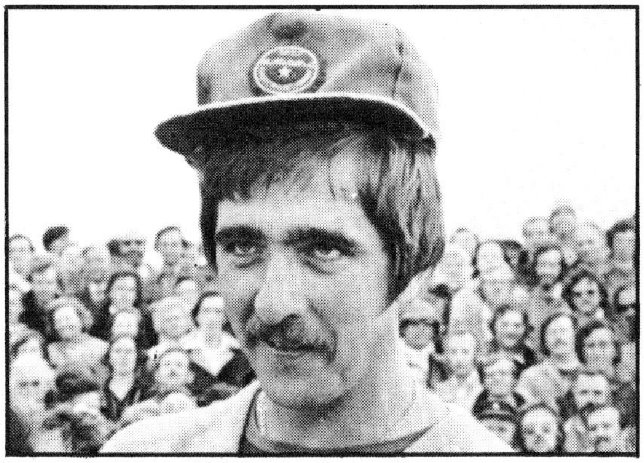

Peter Palmer, Witham champion.

Witham Joint Championships, Witham: Peter Palmer, Nottingham, 11lb 11oz.
West Norfolk Championships, Middle Level: K Jeary, King's Lynn, 1lb 2oz.
Lee Championships: P Horley, Bromages, 11lb 14½oz.

Upper Bristol Avon Championships: I Hornby, Bristol, 5lb 3oz.
Hamilton Taverns/Castle AC open, Grand Union Canal: Paul Barnes, Milton Keynes, 7lb 14oz 6dr.
Crewe and Nantwich Round Table open, Shropshire Union Canal: Monty Foster, Crewe, 7lb 1½oz.
Bedford Hospital Cup, Great Ouse: John Tiddy, St Ives, 91lb 4oz.
Sheffield Works Sports Association Gala, Witham: Ian Bywater, Laycock's, 12lb 15½oz.
Liverpool Post Open, Lancaster Canal: Geoff Holland, Longridge, 6lb 14¼oz.
LAA Geen Cup, Great Ouse: Mick Westby, Stort Valley, 14lb 3oz.
John Haig Whisky Trophy, Middle Level: Jack Speechley, Sheffield, 57lb 5oz.
Tetley Gala, River Welland: Stan Crow, Sheffield, 13lb 2½oz.
William Stones Brewery Gala, River Welland: Bob Goodwin, Travellers, 30lb 14oz.
CISWO Gala, River Welland: Paul Morris, Kellingley Colliery, 12lb 8oz.
Star Green 'Un and Mansfield Brewery, Middle Level: Wayne Martin, Sheffield, 14lb 1oz.

Parks Festival champion, Paul Downes.

Birmingham Parks Festival: Individual Final: Paul Downes, Starlets. Team Champions: Starlets.
BAA Welfare, Middle Severn: John Bishop, Park Lane AC, 10lb 12¼oz.
BAA Welfare, Lower Severn: Roy Marlow, Circle AC, 29lb 15½oz.
BAA Welfare, Middle Severn: Malcolm Wright, Alrewas, 41lb 13½oz.
BAA H Samuels, Staffs/Worcester Canal: Steve Webb, Starlets, 4lb 0½oz.

The Big Matches

BAA Team Championships, Severn: Amblecote. Individual: Terry Walker, Amblecote, 44lb 12oz.
BAA Annual Canal Contest, Birmingham/ Worcester Canal: Ron Baker, West End, 5lb 14½oz.
BAA Big 'Un, Severn, Warwickshire Avon: Bob Miller, Bromsgrove, 44lb 10oz.
NFA Southern Region Championships, Grand Union Canal: M Giordana, 5lb 11oz. Team: Gophers.
NFA London and S East Region Championships, River Wey: Charlie Baldock, Tonbridge A, 14lb 8¼oz. Team: Tonbridge A.
NFA N East Region Championships, Yorkshire Ouse: David Wolstenholme, Slaithwaite, 52lb 12oz.
NFA N West Region Championships, Leeds/Liverpool Canal: John Johnson, Liverpool, 9lb 8oz 6dr. Team: Liverpool.

Paul Evans, NFA Regional champion.

NFA West Midlands Region Championships, Grand Union Canal: Paul Evans, BAA, 5lb. Team: Kidderminster DAA.
NFA Eastern Region Shield, Great Ouse: Nigel Baxter, Rushden, 8lb 14oz. Team: Newport Pagnell.
CIU West Midlands Championships, Warwickshire Avon: C Stewart, Aston Manor, 7lb 15oz. Team: West End.
CIU N West Metropolitan Championships, River Welland: Terry Freeman, Leslie's Catpack, 38lb 5oz.
CIU Leeds Championships, River Wharfe: Paul Werrett, Doncaster, 8lb 13oz. Team: Hall Road WMC.
CIU Wolverhampton Individual Championships, Shropshire Union Canal: Ian Bristow, West End, 1lb 11½oz.

CIU Doncaster Championships, River Witham: John Smith, Wragby Road, 9lb 13oz. Team: Wragby Road.
CIU S Yorks Championships, River Welland: Ray Moss, Rotherham, 33lb 15oz. Team: Aldwark Road C.
CIU Leeds Annual, Wharfe: Phil Wilson, Kirkstall, 6lb 13oz. Team: West Leeds WMC.
CIU National, River Welland: Bert Simmill, Bloxwich, 21lb 14½oz. Team: Coventry Howitzer.
CIU Northern Championships, River Witham: Barry Rodgers, Mexborough, 35lb 10¾oz. Team: Mexborough.
Wye Team Championships: Coleshill. Individual: John Teague, Ross, 12lb 13½oz.
Bristol Avon Team Championships: Stephen's Talisman. Individual: Rod Hill, Stephen's Talisman, 19lb 2½oz.
LAA Shield Final, Thames, Egham: Jubilee beat Defiant Mobile.

Ladies National champion, Avis Thomas.

NFA Ladies' National, River Nene: Avis Thomas, Leeds, 2lb 7oz.
NFA Junior National, Leeds/Liverpool Canal: Alan Hunt, Coventry, 8lb 4oz. Team: Stockport.
Lee Junior Championships: Greg White, Leicester, 3lb 13oz. Team: Leicester B.
N Ireland Schools National, Lough Erne, Enniskillen: Julian McGauley, Newry, 9lb 10oz. Team: St. Malacky's College.
Angling Times Kingfisher Guild Danish Championships, River Skjern: David Davoll, London, 38lb 4oz.
NJAA Championships, Lancaster Canal: David Wiltshire, Stockport, 1lb 14oz 11dr. Team: Stockport.
Angling Times Kingfisher Guild National, Ramsey Forty Foot: Geoffrey Brierley, Oldham, 13lb 12oz.

Embassy Final

In the most dramatic finish in the history of the competion former National champion, Bryan Lakey, snatched the £3,000 first prize from the clutches of last year's winner, Ivan Marks.

At the weigh-in a mere 3lb 3oz separated the two anglers and left the Leicester angler ruefully reflecting on the one extra bream that would have ensured his entry in the record books as the only angler to win the competition twice.

Wisbech angler Bryan scaled 77lb 6oz of bream from his fast-flowing swim on the River Guden at Silkeborg, Denmark while Ivan had a mixed catch of roach and bream for 74lb 3oz.

Bryan, a gentleman's outfitter, clinched the match in the final ten minutes, taking three bream on successive casts. He drew an unfancied peg which he tackled with quivertipped double worm and maggot. Last year's Final, in which he was pegged next to third-placed John Illingworth but failed to break double-figures himself, made him determined to go for bream from the start.

Bombarding his swim with maggot-laced white groundbait, he took fish from the start. "I was shattered at the end of it all, but it really was tremendous to add this win to my success in the 1970 National", he said.

The match followed a different pattern for Ivan Marks. The Leicester tackle dealer started on the float, fishing some slack water near the far bank. After two hours, with just a few roach and a bream, he switched to the tip, offering worm, maggots and casters on the hook. The bream began to feed with a vengeance and with just half an hour to go Ivan was in the lead. But he failed to get another fish before the whistle and had to be content with second place and £1,000.

Third place went to Geoff Lane of York with a bream catch of 52lb 1oz. But his catch would have been even heavier had it not been for a sunken snag in his swim which cost him at least eight bream and a chance of the winner's cheque.

Howard Robson of Leeds took fourth spot with 49lb 5oz of bream. The decision of the organisers to switch the match from October to May in a bid to improve even further the massive returns from the river, proved to be unsuccessful.

The Guden was carrying several feet of snow water and weights were down on previous finals.

Several feet of floodwater turned the Embassy Final into a dour struggle for many of the competitors.

Fourteen anglers failed to weigh in and five others, in the 80-strong field, failed to break the 1lb mark.

Results:

1 B Lakey, Wisbech, 77lb 6oz, £3,000; 2 I Marks, Leicester, 74lb 3oz, £1,000; 3 G Lane, York, 52lb 1oz, £500; 4 H Robson, Leeds, 49lb 5oz, £250; 5 B Newman, Steyning, 40lb 7½oz, £200; 6 P Chadwick, Bedford, 40lb 2½oz, £150; 7 L Sanders, Harleston, 38lb 4oz, £125; 8 W Bullock, Hayes and Harlington, 37lb 4½oz, £100; 9 B Orchard, Reading, 35lb 13oz, £75; 10 M Holbrook, Bristol and West, 32lb 1½oz, £50; 11 J McCarthy, Steyning, 28lb 2oz, £45; 12 B Wright, Hull, 27lb 8½oz, £40; 13 R Hill, Bath, 26lb 6½oz, £35; 14 J Marcer, Long Eaton, 21lb 6oz, £30; 15 V Foster, Long Eaton, 18lb 2oz, £25; 16 D Vincent, Hayes and Harlington, 17lb 6½oz; 17 M Webb, Leeds, 15lb 15oz; 18 K Hornsey, Cardiff, 15lb 8oz; 19 T Stothers, Ashton, 14lb 7½oz; 20 B Mallory, Tadcaster, 13lb 12oz; 21 A Ackroyd, Bramley, 13lb 11oz; 22 R Jordan, Doncaster, 13lb 5oz; 23 M Kirk, Oxford, 13lb 4oz; 24 D Kirk, Oxford, 13lb; 25 D Browning, Coventry, 12lb 6½oz; 26 J Kelly, Northwich, 10lb 6oz; 27 G Scollick, Bradford City, 10lb 1oz; 28 R Disley, Upper Ouse, 9lb 4oz; 29 D Wyatt, S Davall, 9lb 3½oz; 30 M Leask, Tonbridge, 8lb 11oz.

Previous Winners:

1968: Coombe Abbey Lake, Kevin Ashurst, Leigh, 31lb 12¼oz.
1969: Coombe Abbey Lake, E Wilde, Swinton, 10lb 10oz.
1970: River Blackwater, E Townsin, Cambridge, 43lb 4oz.
1971: Guden, J Parsons, Leeds, 80lb 5¼oz.
1972: Guden, M Wrigglesworth, Guiseley, 125lb 8oz.
1973: Guden, C Love, London, 71lb 14oz.
1974: Guden, J Dempster, Gloucester, 80lb 3oz.
1975: Guden, K Giles, Birmingham, 110lb 5oz.
1976: Guden, D White, Rochdale, 74lb 1½oz.
1977: Guden, I Marks, Leicester, 110lb 7oz.

Winner Bryan Lakey nets yet another bream.

Runner-up Ivan Marks with his 74lb 3oz catch.

20
KING SIZE
Embassy
Number 1
Embassy
Number 1
EIK/67S

Ken Giles

Mr Unflappable

For the last twenty years the name of Ken Giles has dominated match fishing headlines throughout the country. The Birmingham angler is now one of the best known, and most respected, figures on the match angling circuit.

His record of success is second to none and he has chalked up hundreds of wins on every conceivable type of water, ranging from the shallow Midland canals to the wide, windswept, bream rivers of Eastern England. And Ken's consistency is such that he will undoubtedly figure among the very top flight of match anglers for at least another decade.

He has been an angler ever since he can remember and was still in short pants when he began his match fishing career. His first tutor was his uncle, a friend of that legendary match ace, Benny Ashurst. Ken often accompanied his uncle on visits to Lancashire — visits that gave him the chance to watch, and fish with, the great Benny Ashurst.

His next tutor was Albert Rodway, the greatest Birmingham angler of his day. Says Ken: "I was a hanger-on really. I followed Albert to all the matches, and that meant a lot of travelling. There were far fewer big opens in those days and it meant I had to travel all over the country to watch, and fish against, the top men."

Those travels took him far from his local rivers, the Severn and Warwickshire Avon, but they gave him first hand experience of the other major match rivers in the country — the Trent, Witham, Welland, Nene and Thames.

Ken's main ambition at that time was to represent the mighty Birmingham team in the National Championships. That chance came in 1961, on the River Trent. Since that year Ken has been a regular member of the team, and has now fished 19 consecutive Nationals.

But although Ken won match after match during the Sixties he was rarely accorded the recognition he deserved. His fellow top matchmen were full of admiration for his skills. But he was in danger of becoming 'the professionals' Professional', never quite achieving his rightful national acclaim.

He is by nature a modest, quietly-spoken man, a true gentleman of the match circuit. Had he been a more flamboyant character recognition may well have come sooner.

Ken had to wait until 1973 before the angling world finally realised he had arrived. In that year he was picked by the England manager Stan Smith to fish in the World Championships in France.

Ken Giles — a world class matchman.

It was Ken's big chance and he seized it with both hands. His performance in the match was superb. The mass of spectators which gathered behind his peg didn't need much angling knowledge to realise that they were watching a great angler in action.

For three hours, despite the tremendous mental pressures and despite the limited-line ruling which handicapped every England team man, he gave a truly brilliant display. Every cast was inch-perfect, every movement was swift, yet unhurried.

He was coolness personified — a flawless match-fishing machine. On a day when many other great world stars failed to impress he finished sixth individual. Had he not lost a huge perch which stripped the fifteen metres of line, the maximum amount allowed in the rules, from his reel, he would have been world champion.

Since that day Ken has fished twice more for England and it remains a mystery to many anglers why he has not become a regular member of the squad.

But success has certainly not eluded him in recent years. He won the richest prize in angling — the £3,000 Embassy Challenge Final in 1975 with yet another unflappable display of silky skill. And in 1978 he won the Angling Times League Final individual title with more than 60lb of bream from Coombe Abbey.Lake, Coventry.

Not only is he a great individual angler, he is also a superb team man. As a member of both the Birmingham national team and the Cofton Hackett match group he has won every major team honour in the book.

He has helped the Birmingham squad to three National wins in the last seven years and Cofton Hackett have won the Angling Times League Final now fewer than four times.

Team fishing is all about sharing knowledge and comradeship with fellow anglers — factors that rank at the top of Ken's priorities.

"Fishing, whether it be match fishing or pleasure, is all about enjoyment. Winning money is an added bonus but the true matchman fishes for pleasure. I've always wanted to be a matchman and I get as much pleasure from it now as when I first took up the sport."

"I've made dozens of life-long friends through the sport and I can't ever imagine a time when I would pack up my rods and stop fishing."

At the age of 42 Ken still has plenty of years left in the top flight. And he has some useful advice for the crop of youngsters now competing on the open circuit.

"The youngster must always remember that he will never know it all. A few open wins won't turn him into a world beater overnight. The casualty list of good youngsters who have fallen by the wayside without ever realising their potential is enormous. The youngster must keep everything in perspective, looking to learn from every match he fishes."

"There are no short cuts to the top, just hard work and hours of practice. The young angler must have the tenacity to want to succeed. All the tuition in the world is useless if you can't really be bothered to put in the hours on these routine things that are essential to success. And, above all, the youngster must fish matches because, win or lose, that's what he enjoys most of all. Once the enjoyment goes he might as well throw his tackle in the dustbin."

Ken unhooks a perch on his way to sixth place in the 1973 World Championships.

Benson and Hedges Festival

A final day burst saw outsider Bill Reade of Stockport carry off the winner's £1,000 cheque in the Benson and Hedges Festival on the River Erne.

After two of the three matches Bill was well behind the star-studded field, trailing the leaders by nearly 50lb. But the final match proved decisive with Bill scaling 101lb 4½oz of bream to take third place on the day and give him first prize overall with an aggregate of 214lb 3½oz.

The win came as a big surprise to the 33 year-old service engineer. He won his section in the first match with 79lb 12oz but seemed to have dropped out of the running when he drew a bad peg in the second event and could weigh in only 32lb 12oz. His final peg was in yet another unfancied area but a shoal of bream was in residence and Bill's ability with the pole did the rest. Together with his success in the first match Bill totalled £1,400 in prize money.

Second place, and a cheque for £800, went to Ivan Hancock of Stoke-on-Trent. Hairdresser Ivan had a slow start to the series taking catches of 48lb 0½oz and 36lb 10oz in the first two matches. But he won the final match with 119lb 15½oz of bream to aggregate 205lb. Third place went to Chelmsford angler Peter Clapperton who picked up £600 for a total of 203lb 11½oz. Peter won the opening match with 109lb 2oz and took 26lb 6oz and 68lb 3½oz in the final events.

Unluckiest man in the field was Cheshunt, Herts angler Dickie Carr, who led the field with 160lb 6oz after two matches. A bad draw in the final match saw him struggle for 21lb 12oz and he eventually finished sixth overall and just out of the prize money.

Although individual catches failed to reach the peaks of the previous two years' events, mainly due to the cold spring weather, catches still averaged out at 92lb per angler — sensational fishing by any standards.

Results:

First Day:
1 P Clapperton, Chelmsford, 109lb 2oz; 2 2 A Sellars, Sheffield, 99lb 15oz; 3 D Carr, Cheshunt, 94lb 15oz; 4 H Pattison, Dublin, 92lb 10oz; 5 W Reade, Stockport, 79lb 12oz; 6 P Dudley, Nottingham, 78lb 2oz.

Second Day:
1 K Hobson, Barnsley, 121lb 5oz; 2 W Beard, Wrexham, 118lb 6oz; 3 D Stewart, Enniskillen, 105lb; 4 P Cuniffe, Oldham, 98lb 1½oz.

Bill Reade of Stockport holds one of the bream that clinched the £1,000 first prize in the Benson and Hedges Festival. Bill totalled £1,400 for his overall win.

Third Day:
1 I Hancock, Stoke-on-Trent, 119lb 15½oz; 2 S Gardener, Redhill, 106lb 2½oz; 3 W Reade, Stockport, 101lb 4½oz; 4 J Sheppard, Lancaster, 88lb 11oz.

Overall Result:
1 W Reade, Stockport, £1,000, 214lb 3½oz; 2 I Hancock, Stoke-on-Trent, £800, 205lb; 3 P Clapperton, Chelmsford, £600, 203lb 11½oz; 4 S Gardener, Redhill, £400, 197lb 6oz; 5 K Hobson, Barnsley, £200, 190lb 8oz; 6 D Carr, Cheshunt, 182lb 2oz; 7 B Nudd, Chelmsford, 181lb 12½oz; 8 W Beard, Wrexham, 173lb 14½oz; 9 P Dudley, Nottingham, 167lb 13oz; 10 S O'Rourke, Essex and P Ottewill, Croydon, both 158lb 2oz.

Despite this superb 80lb catch of roach ex-Sheffield angler Keith Boswell still failed to figure among the winners of the festival — proof of the superb quality of the fishing.

MIDDLE TAR As defined by H.M. Government
H.M. Government Health Departments' WARNING:
CIGARETTES CAN SERIOUSLY DAMAGE YOUR HEALTH

Irish Match Fishing

Fermanagh Festival

The world five hour match catch record was elevated to a new peak when Norfolk angler Dennis Willis put a staggering 207lb 8oz of fish on the scales in the opening match of the Fermanagh Festival.

Electronics engineer Dennis hammered out 200lb of roach, together with a few bream and hybrids, from his peg on the Erne at Enniskillen. All the fish fell to pole tactics coupled with 4lb line, size 10 hook and bunches of maggots.

Needless to say the huge weight gave Dennis a comfortable lead over second placed Dave Stuart, who weighed in 145lb 7½oz and third placed Ian Heaps who totalled 132lb 8½oz.

The second match provided another crop of 'ton up' weights and proved crucial to the eventual outcome of the festival. Ian Heaps turned in yet another brilliant performance to take the honours with 161lb 15oz — a catch that might easily have topped the 200lb mark had it not been for a difficult bank at Ian's peg which forced him to stand, knee-deep in water for most of the match.

Ian lost nearly 40lb of fish, which dropped off the hook as he was landing them, an incident which could easily have proved crucial to the overall result. Second place went to Stockport's Tony Knight, with 159lb 7oz with Chester's John Tyreman third with 140lb 8½oz.

The final match proved to be the real decider and another 100lb catch from Heaps was enough to give him the championship outright. Ian weighed in 118lb 10oz, and although it didn't even put him in the top six places it was more than enough as his closest rivals faltered.

Leicester's Alan Bray won the last match with 152lb 5oz, followed by Barry Rudge of Goole with 147lb 15oz and local angler Gordon Dickinson with 127lb 12oz.

But Ian's nearest rivals, Dennis Willis and Tony Knight both faltered leaving Ian a clear outright winner with an aggregate of 413lb 1½oz. Dennis Willis had the consolation of second place to add to his world record, thanks to an aggregate of 331lb 9½oz with Gordon Fletcher third with 302lb 13oz.

Results:

Match one:
1 Dennis Willis, 207lb 8oz; 2 Dave Stuart, 145lb 7½oz; 3 Ian Heaps, 132lb 8½oz.

Match Two:
1 Ian Heaps, 161lb 15oz; 2 Tony Knight, 159lb 7oz; 3 John Tyreman, 140lb 8½oz; 4 Roy Meredith, 133lb 4oz; 5 Gordon Fletcher, 118lb 2oz; 6 Gerry Hartley, 103lb 12oz.

Match Three:
1 Alan Bray, 152lb 5oz; 2 Barry Rudge, 147lb 15oz; 3 Gordon Dickinson, 127lb 12oz; 4 Ron Goodacre, 125lb 4oz; 5 Tony Farrington, 121lb 2oz; 6 Gordon Fletcher, 120lb 11oz.

Overall:
1 Ian Heaps, 413lb 1½oz; 2 Dennis Willis, 331lb 9½oz; 3 Gordon Fletcher, 302lb 13oz; 4 Ron Goodacre, 295lb 4oz; 5 Tony Knight, 274lb 11oz; 6 Barry Rudge, 272lb 6oz.

Prosperous Festival

Irishman Norman Howarth plucked the honours and £675 of prize money from the grasp of a star-studded field of English aces in the three match Prosperous Festival.

And Carrickmacross angler Norman did it despite a disastrous first match in which he could weigh only 1lb 2oz, almost 30lb behind the leaders.

The honours in that first match, on the Grand Canal at Prosperous, went to St Helens, Lancs angler, Joe Lee with 31lb 1oz of bream. Dave Hopkin of Blackpool was second with 29lb 15oz, followed by Jamie Kenny of Normanton with 21lb 0½oz.

The second match turned into a peg-for-peg battle between Barry Rudge of Goole and Jamie Kenny as they shared the same bream shoal. Barry eventually took top spot with 27lb 14oz but Jamie's second placed 24lb 4oz put him into a clear overall lead. Third place in the match went to

Dennis Willis — the new world record holder.

Norman Howarth with 24lb 3oz.

The final match saw the best weights of the Festival with London angler Mick Giordano scaling 50lb 7oz of bream despite having the shoal scattered by a passing boat. That weight alone would have been enough to give him the overall honours, had it not been for Norman who took third place with 31lb 5oz — a decisive catch.

Mick Giordano had only taken 3lb 7oz in the two previous matches and had to be content with a three day aggregate of 53lb 14oz, and second place behind Norman's aggregate of 56lb 10oz. Third place overall went to Jamie Kenny with 47lb 4oz. The team prize went to Norman's team, Springtippers with a total of 113lb 7oz. Runners up were St Helens Ospreys with 94lb 13oz.

Results:

Match One:
1 J Lee, St Helens, 31lb 1oz; 2 D Hopkin, Blackpool, 29lb 15oz; 3 J Kenny, Normanton, 21lb 0½oz; 4 T Boulton, Norwich, 18lb.

Match Two:
1 B Rudge, Goole, 27lb 14oz; 2 J Kenny, Normanton, 24lb 4oz; 3 N Howarth, Carrickmacross, 24lb 3oz; 4 N Farrell, Prosperous, 21lb 11oz.

Match Three:
1 M Giordano, London, 50lb 7oz; 2 D Clark, Wigan, 43lb 14oz; 3 N Howarth, Carrickmacross, 31lb 5oz; 4 F Latham, Nantwich, 24lb 3oz.

Overall:
1 N Howarth, 56lb 10oz; 2 M Giordano, 53lb 14oz; 3 J Kenny, 47lb 4oz.

Fermanagh victor, Ian Heaps.

Teams:
1 Springtippers, 113lb 7oz; 2 St Helens Ospreys, 94lb 13oz.

Ballinasloe Festival

The 1979 Ballinasloe Festival provided yet another triumph for the 'Academy', the Wisbech, Cambs match group. The 'Academy' took the team honours for the third successive year and also provided the overall individual winner, Syd Meads junior, son of the previous year's winner, Syd Meads senior.

The river Suck fished poorly in the opening two matches but catches did improve in the final match. It was this match that clinched the winnings for young Syd — he won it with 43lb 11oz of bream to push his three day aggregate to 52lb 5oz.

Results:

Individual:
1 S Meads jnr, 52lb 5oz; 2 D Hall, Bogthorpe Herons, 31lb 12oz; 3 G Casey, Roding Valley, 27lb 8oz; 4 M Mobbs, Huntingdon, 26lb 4oz; 5 S Warner, Bogthorpe Herons, 22lb 9oz; 6 B Weeks, Bathampton, 20lb 5oz.

Teams:
1 Academy, 64lb 12oz; 2 Bogthorpe Hersons, 57lb 6oz; 3 Bathampton, 46lb 8oz; 4 Mad Trio, 45lb 6oz; 5 Izaak Walton One, 39lb 3oz; 6 Roding Valley, 31lb 14oz.

Syd Meads junior, Ballinasloe winner.

Pike Championships

Two pike for 22lb 3oz made Norfolk draughtsman, John Heard, 1979 British Pike Champion. But it was no runaway victory for the 26 year-old St German's angler — rumours were sweeping the bank, before the final whistle, about a 20 pounder which had been taken by another angler.

The rumour turned into reality as Denham, Bucks angler Fred Holloway put a massive fish on the scales. The pike was the largest of the match. But at 20lb 12oz it wasn't quite large enough to win and John was able to breathe a sigh of relief.

John qualified for the match twice — once on the draw at a fishless qualifier and again at the Swanton Morley qualifier. He tackled his swim, at the Denver Sluice end of the Great Ouse at Ten Mile Bank, with a link-legered roach deadbait. His first pike, a fish of 9¼lb, was taken in the opening 40 minutes of the match.

A delighted John Heard displays one of the two pike that helped clinch the 1979 British Pike Championships on the Great Ouse.

A second, finicky, take on a similar rig, half-way through the match, really sewed it all up. John's strike connected with a 12lb 15oz fish and the championship was his.

Second place went to Fred Holloway with his superb 20 pounder. Fred took his fish on legered sprat at a peg between Windmill Bridge and the Engine pump. It battled for 20 minutes before being landed and was Fred's first-ever 20 pounder.

Although he sat for the rest of the match without another bite, Fred was far from unhappy. "To catch a 20 pounder has made the trip worthwhile", he said.

Third place went to Steve Dyett of Slough, Bucks, with a single fish of 14lb 3oz and two anglers fishing adjacent pegs opposite the Brandon Creek outfall took fourth and fifth places. Trevor Preston from Nottingham landed a 13lb 8½oz fish to scrape home ahead of David Leah of Preston, Lancs who landed a single fish of 13lb 2½oz.

With a cold wind scything across the match length catches were lower than expected. Few zander were caught despite claims by local matchmen that the match stretch was full of them. Best zander of the day, at 3lb 11½oz, fell to the link-legered roach deadbait of Bud Collie of Newark.

Results:

1 J Heard, 22lb 3oz; 2 F Holloway, 20lb 12oz; 3 S Dyett, 14lb 3oz; 4 T Preston, 13lb 8½oz; 5 D Leah, 13lb 6½oz; 6 P Ward, 11lb 1oz; 7 I Holliday, 8lb 12oz; 8 W Beilby, 8lb 0½oz; 9 T Hattley, 7lb 11oz; 10 K Walters, 7lb 7½oz; 11 R Mumford, 6lb 9oz; 12 T Probyn, 6lb 8¾oz.

Sections:
Pegs 1-50: 1 S Dyett; 2 J Scott-Telford, 5lb 11oz; 51-100: 1 R Mumford; 2 J Swann, 5lb 1oz; 101-150: 1 P Rix, 4lb 6½oz; 2 A Obey, 4lb 4oz; 151-200: 1 J Heard; 2 F Holloway. 201-250: 1 E Wright, 6lb 6½oz; 2 T Sharratt, 6lb. 251-300: 1 W Beilby; 2 T Probyn. 301-350: 1 P Ward; 2 S Girvan, 3lb 2oz. 351-400: 1 T Preston; 2 D Leah.

Zander:
1 A Collie, 3lb 11½oz; 2 C Loveland, 3lb 3oz; 3 R Ramsey, 2lb 3oz.

The Angling Times Winter League

Robin Harris and Roger Brierley celebrate their Final battle with a handshake.

Peter James of Downton who took fourth place in the Final with 37lb 8oz.

Southern semi-final

The Southern semi-final once again produced a sensational result which turned the form book inside out. As so often in the past, the red-hot favourites failed to make any impact and it was the outsiders who grabbed the glory.

The Crown Fishery, on the River Lee at Broxbourne, was in a far from accommodating mood — carrying extra, coloured, water and lashed by an icy East wind. But the two favourite sides, Simpson's ABC and Catpack Daiwa, just couldn't find their form and slumped to tenth and eleventh places respectively with less than 8oz of fish between them.

Instead it was a day of smiles for the bookmaker and outsiders, King Heron, Isfield and Oundle. King Heron, the Berkshire champions, made the largest impact, taking the team award with 6lb 10¼oz and providing the individual match winner in Dave Breame.

King Heron had only three men weigh in but Dave Breame's winning individual weight — four chub for 5lb 1¼oz — was enough to guarantee them the match. Drawn at a hotly-fancied peg, opposite a moored barge, Swindon angler Dave fished the far bank with the waggler and single bronze maggot on a size 20 hook. His match-winning catch, of fish to 1½lb, was taken from a four-feet deep swim.

Second team spot went to Sussex champions, Isfield, making their first semi-final appearance. Most of the side had fished the river regularly and, from the opening whistle, team tactics were to concentrate on the chub shoals. The bulk of the side's 4lb 11¼oz total was provided by team captain, Brian Wickens, who took second individual place with a chub and three small roach for 2lb 5½oz.

But there were invaluable contributions of 1lb 3oz and 13½oz from fellow team members Stewart Cottingham and Derek Strippe. The third Final place was decided in the closing 15 minutes of the match. It looked odds-on that Kent side, 279AC, would qualify for the Final . . . until Oundle angler, Chris Cooper, hooked a plump chub with his first bite of the day. After a few anxious moments the fish was safely netted and at 2lb 1¼oz was enough to give him third individual place. More important, it boosted his side's team total to 3lb 15¼oz, just six ounces clear of 279.

For the Oundle side it was quite a performance. Although they included many star names, they had never fished the water before and their performance left captain Peter Lee, who played a major part in helping his team through with a weight of 1lb 7oz, absolutely delighted. For 279, it was yet another disappointment. In the previous season's semi-final they had been beaten into fourth place by just 3oz!

There was disappointment too for reigning Winter League champions, Dorking. Hard as they fished they could finish only fifth with 2lb 9¼oz.

Results:

Teams:
1 King Heron, 6lb 10¼oz; 2 Isfield, 4lb 11¼oz; 3 Oundle, 3lb 15¼oz; 4 279AC, 3lb 9oz; 5 Dorking, 2lb 9¼oz; 6 Maidstone, 2lb 9oz; 7 East Hampstead, 1lb 12¼oz; 8 Deben, 7oz; 9 Defiant Mobile, 6½oz; 10 Simpson's ABC, 5¼oz; 11 Catpack Daiwa, 2½oz.

Individuals:
1 D Breame, King Heron, 5lb 1¼oz; 2 B Wickens, Isfield, 2lb 5½oz; 3 C Cooper, Oundle, 2lb 1¼oz; 4 J Sene, 279AC, 1lb 13oz; 5 M Richardson, Dorking, 1lb 11oz; 6 D Goldsmith, Maidstone, 1lb 10¾oz.

David Breame of King Heron nets another chub on his way to victory.

Northern semi-final

The Northern semi-final turned into a real cliff-hanger of an event as teams struggled to pit their skill against a raging river Trent. With the river, at Gunthorpe Bridge, carrying nearly four foot extra of coloured snow-water, the outcome was in the balance right up to the final whistle.

A solitary chub or sizeable roach would have been enough to put any one of the eleven teams on their way to the Final in Ireland. And, not surprisingly, the eventual result produced yet more upsets for the form book.

Pre-match red-hot favourites, Trentman, slumped to tenth place, beaten by the conditions and not lack of skill. In contrast, one of the outsiders, Leeds C, a team which had qualified for the semi-final by a mere quarter of an ounce, not only carried off the team honours but supplied the top individual too.

Yarm A, the North East outfit who had finished second in the previous semi-final, made it a double by taking second place again and the North's most consistent side, Deva, made it their fourth Final appearance on the trot by sneaking home in third place.

Leeds' success hinged almost entirely on the efforts of young Jim Jordan, drawn at peg 94. Jim stuck to pre-match tactics, running a stick float and chrysodine maggot combination through his six foot deep swim. He took a 12oz roach in the opening minutes of the match and had only two more bites during the match. But he made the most of them to weigh in a trio of plump roach for 2lb 4oz. Only three of his team mates weighed in to give the side a total of 2lb 7½oz — a meagre weight but enough for a comfortable victory.

Individual winner Jim Jordan of Leeds also clinched a Final place for his team.

At the next peg to Jim was Yarm angler Mick Grainge. Mick followed team tactics and started with a float leger rig fished under the pole. But he soon switched to a stick float and was rewarded with a brace of roach for 1lb 13oz and second individual spot. Mick's weight was enough to put his side into second team place but Yarm's total was boosted to 2lb 0½oz by contributions from three other team men.

The third and last place in the Final developed into a nail-biting battle between experienced Deva and Eastern champions, Grimsby. Deva, one of the most experienced teams in the match, were in their element, scratching hard for fish. Bob Serge played a real captain's part by taking a 1lb chub and sixth individual place on his only bite of the day. Keith Bean and John Tyreman contributed 1 and 1½oz respectively; John Jackson weighed in a priceless 7oz of gudgeon, and two other team members took a gudgeon apiece to push the side's total to 1lb 10½oz.

Grimsby captain, Geoff Allison, also fished magnificently to take third individual place with a solitary chub of 1lb 5¼oz. Two of his team mates also weighed in but the final team tally was 1lb 10oz, a gudgeon short of a place in the Final.

Fifth place went to Lancashire giants, Crusaders, led by mighty Kevin Ashurst. Kevin provided the bulk of his team's 1lb 5¾oz total with a solitary bream of 1lb 1¼oz, a fish that also gave him fourth individual spot.

Fifth individual was Brian Davies of Connah's Quay with 1lb 0½oz of bleak from peg 131. Brian's catch helped his side to 1lb 5½oz and sixth team place.

Results:

Teams:
1 Leeds C, 2lb 7½oz; 2 Yarm A, 2lb 0½oz; 3 Deva, 1lb 10½oz; 4 Grimsby, 1lb 10oz; 5 Crusaders, 1lb 5¾oz; 6 Connah's Quay, 1lb 5½oz; 7 Leek and Morelands, 14¾oz; 8 Cammel Laird, 10¼oz; 9 Harraton, 8½oz; 10 Trentman, 7oz; 11 Little Lever, 3¾oz.

Individuals:
1 J Jordan, Leeds, 2lb 4oz; 2 M Grainge, Yarm, 1lb 13oz; 3 G Allison, Grimsby, 1lb 5¼oz; 4 K Ashurst, Crusaders, 1lb 1¼oz; 5 B Davies, Connah's Quay, 1lb 0½oz; 6 B Serge, Deva, 1lb.

Midland semi-final

A burst of action in the closing stages of the match saw Birmingham's Starlets side record their third successive semi-final victory in the Midland event on the Thames at Dorchester.

The side's success was almost entirely due to skipper Barry Fulford, and a change of tactics in the final 90 minutes of the match. Barry, drawn two pegs above the Thame mouth, switched his feeder-rig tactics to a far bank swim after seeing the man above him, Cofton's Paul Evans, land a chub from that line. His first bite produced a foul-hooked pike of 2½lb, and he followed it with a brace of plump chub, both of which fell to double bronze maggot. Barry's final total was 8lb 9oz, enough for a runaway individual victory, and a weight that boosted his side's total to 10lb 4¾oz.

Big fish dominated the match as the low water temperature put the smaller fish completely off the feed. Concentration for the all-important bites was the keystone of team success on a day on which the fancied teams failed to impress. Outsiders, LMS, the Shropshire champions, took second place with a fine display of single-minded concentration.

Drawn next to the hotly-fancied Ensor's side, a team boasting Ivan Marks, Phil Coles and Roy Marlow, they were far from over-awed. Ray Harris was their top weight and fourth individual with a single barbel of 4lb 6¼oz, landed after a 15 minute fight on a size 20 hook and 1lb line. Team mate Mick Williams contributed a chub of 2lb 11oz and the team total was boosted to 8lb 15¾oz by a 1lb 14½oz chub from Ron Yeomans.

The biggest upset of the day was provided by lowly Downton, the tiny Wiltshire club which had never before reached a semi-final. The team caught only two fish, but together they weighed 8lb.

Roger Moody led the way with a barbel of 4lb 7½oz, taken on a lobworm fished on a size 8 hook. And had he not lost a much larger barbel Downton's performance would have been even more impressive. Another Moody, team captain Arthur, provided the rest of the weight with a bream of 3lb 8¾oz, only the second bream he had ever caught!

Unluckiest team of the day were South West champions, Portcullis. Their captain, Roger Sheppard, turned in one of the best individual performances of the match, taking second individual place with 4lb 8oz of roach. Roger took 15 fish on small worms, legered on a size 18 hook, and, had he landed a pike which grabbed a roach as he was reeling it in, his side would have qualified for the Final. Instead his teammates could only add 2lb 11oz leaving the side tantalisingly close in fourth spot.

The local Kidlington side took fifth spot with 6lb 2oz and Ensor's and Farnborough shared sixth place with 5lb 13oz apiece.

Results:

Individuals:
1 B Fulford, Starlets, 8lb 9oz; 2 R Sheppard, Portcullis, 4lb 8oz; 3 R Moody, Downton, 4lb 7½oz; 4 R Harris, LMS, 4lb 6¼oz; 5 P St Leger, ATS Kingfishers, 3lb 9½oz; 6 A Moody, Downton, 3lb 8¾oz.

Teams:
1 Starlets, 10lb 4¾oz; 2 LMS, 8lb 15¾oz; 3 Downton, 8lb 0¼oz; 4 Portcullis, 7lb 3oz; 5 Kidlington, 6lb 2oz; 6 Farnborough and Ensor's, both 5lb 13oz; 8 ATS Kingfishers, 5lb 4oz; 9 Cofton Hackett, 4lb 2½oz; 10 Bridgewater 4½oz.

Jubilant Starlets celebrate their second successive semi-final victory.

Final

Unfancied Isfield sprang one of the biggest surprises in Winter League history by snatching the title from right under the noses of the red-hot favourites. And their stunning victory was no fluke in a thrilling battle on the River Blackwater at Fermoy, Southern Ireland. Competing in their first ever Final they totalled 137lb to finish nearly 13lb clear of their nearest rivals.

The Blackwater, hosting the first Irish Winter League Final for five years, was in fantastic form. The 108 competitors weighed in nearly 800lb of quality roach and dace. Only three of the previous 12 Irish finals have provided heavier team and individual weights — and they were all on bream waters!

But the day really belonged to the outsiders from Sussex. Most of the side had fished the river before and all but one of the team weighed in. Star of the side was reserve Roger Brierley, drafted into the side just a week before the match. Roger weighed in a stunning 56lb 12oz roach and dace — a catch that also pushed him into second individual spot.

But it wasn't a one-man show, there were good backing weights from the rest of the side. Mick Murray contributed 23lb 7oz; seventeen-year-old Lee Murray weighed in 15½lb and Bob Sutherland 12lb 9oz.

Second place went to one of the pre-match favourites, Oundle, who totalled 124lb 1¼oz. Oundle, runners-up in the 1976 Final, had estimated that a team weight of 90lb would win them the match. They made their target with plenty to spare but were disappointed to find it wasn't enough on the day.

Former World and National champion, Robin Harris provided the bulk of the side's weight with 55lb 6oz, and there were good backing weights

Winner Phil King of King Heron with his 61lb 5oz catch.

Second placed Roger Brierley swings a dace to hand during his battle with Robin Harris.

from Geoff King, 10lb 7oz; Andy Putnins, 20lb 8oz and skipper Peter Lee, 10lb 4oz.

Third spot went to another of the more fancied sides, King Heron with a total weight of 122lb 2½oz. The Berkshire side had the consolation of providing the individual winner, Phil King, who weighed in 61lb 5oz. But skipper Arthur Turner was disappointed with his side's placing.

Said Arthur: "I really rated our chances of winning the match. We weighed in far more than our pre-match target weight but it wasn't enough on the day."

Fourth place went to lowly Downton, the tiny Hampshire club who fished magnificently to total 91lb 2½oz. Hot favourites Starlets failed completely, judged by their own high standards, and had to be content with fifth place.

The individual event turned into a four-horse race between the anglers pegged nearest to Fermoy town bridge. Winner Phil King was the first to make contact with the huge shoals of roach and dace and built up a commanding lead as the men below him, Robin Harris of Oundle and Roger Brierley struggled for fish.

But in the last two hours of the match both anglers began to claw back the King Heron tackle dealer's lead as their swims came to life. Feeding heavily with maggots and groundbait the two anglers were taking 12oz dace and roach to 1½lb on virtually every cast.

Robin Harris, clearly well behind both Phil and Roger, turned in an amazing display of speed fishing in the final minutes of the match. But a nail-biting weigh-in saw Phil King emerge as a clear winner with 61lb 5oz, with Roger Brierley pipping Robin Harris for second spot by 56lb 12oz to 55lb 6oz. The fourth man in the line, Peter James of Downton, finished fourth with 37lb 8oz.

The spoils of victory — Winter League Champions, Isfield, display their trophies.

Oundle team man Robin Harris swings in yet another fish on his way to third place.

Results:

Teams:
1 Isfield, 137lb; 2 Oundle, 124lb 1¼oz; 3 King Heron, 122lb 2½oz; 4 Downton, 91lb 2½oz; 5 Starlets, 76lb 10¼oz; 6 LMS, 67lb 1¼oz; 7 Deva, 59lb 9oz; 8 Yarm, 46lb 14½oz; 9 Leeds C, 43lb 1oz.

Individuals:
1 P King, King Heron, 61lb 5oz; 2 R Brierley, Isfield, 56lb 12oz; 3 R Harris, Oundle, 55lb 6oz; 4 P James, Downton, 37lb 8oz; 5 B Hines, Starlets, 24lb 14oz; 6 D Murray, Isfield, 23lb 7oz; 7 B Edwards, LMS, 21lb 10oz; 8 D Lodge, Starlets, 21lb 5oz; 9 A Putnins, Oundle, 20lb 8oz; 10 J Davies, LMS, 16lb 8oz.

Sections:
Pegs 1 to 9: M Thill, King Herón, 3lb 5oz; 10-18: F Jefferson, Oundle, 1lb 5½oz; 19-27: A Hadley, Downton, 12lb 1½oz; 28-36: M Murray, Isfield, 23lb 7oz; 37-45: K Bean, Deva, 15lb 1oz; 46-54: D Lodge, Starlets, 21lb 5oz; 55-63: P King, King Heron, 61lb 5oz; 42-67: B Wilson, Isfield, 4lb; 73-81: M Cottle, King Heron, 9lb 10oz; 82-90: M Spares, King Heron, 9lb 3oz; 91-99: F Moss, Deva, 5lb; 100-108: R Sutherland: Isfield, 12lb 9oz.

League Final Winners

Year	Venue	Individual	Team
1960	Nene	S. Ayre, Lincoln 13¼ oz	Lincoln, 13¼ oz
1961	Nene	B. Weekes, Bathampton 15lb 15¼oz	Bathampton, 15lb 15¼oz
1962	Boyle	P. Reeves, Dartford 7lb 8¼oz	Dartford, 16lb 15¼oz
1963	Finn	M. Skipsey, Thirsk 26lb 1½oz	Leeds, 49lb 14½oz
1964	Suck	K. Ashurst, Leicester 56lb 9oz	Leicester, 145lb 3¼oz
1965	Blackwater	C Naylor, Leicester 19lb 2½oz	Leicester, 79lb 3¾oz
1966	Erne	L. Davies, Cofton Hackett 22lb 15oz	Cofton, 56lb 0½oz
1967	Boyle	J. Dyer, Colebrook 17lb 3oz	Colebrook, 21lb 10½oz
1968	Rinn	J. Ryder, Cofton Hackett 6lb 11½oz	Cofton, 16lb 1½oz
1969	Erne	N. Duncombe, Amery Unionists 6lb 5½oz	Cardiff Nomads, 13lb 4¾oz
1970	Blackwater	J. Garratty, Hunts Anglers 24lb 0½oz	Hunts Anglers, 89lb 6¼oz
1971	Shannon	A. Clissett, Cofton Hackett 101lb 6oz	Cofton, 276lb 13½oz
1972	Great Ouse	N. Randles, Chester 27lb 5½oz	Chester, 59lb 7¾oz
1973	Blackwater	J. Lipscombe, Caustons 20lb 9oz	Rotherham, 49lb 6¼oz
1974	Shannon	C. Paine, Saints 89lb 15oz	Saints, 187lb 9¼oz
1975	Coombe Abbey	K. Sheath, Crawley 8lb 15oz	Crawley, 44lb 7¼oz
1976	Coombe Abbey	K. Smith, Cofton Hackett 30lb 8oz	Cofton, 110lb 6½oz
1977	Coombe Abbey	S. Webb, Starlets 61lb 5oz	Barnsley, 127lb 13oz
1978	Coombe Abbey	K. Giles, Cofton Hackett 60lb 15½oz	Dorking, 169lb 6¾oz

Anglers battle it out in the League Final on the River Blackwater at Fermoy.

The Money Winners

Kevin Ashurst, top money winner of the year.

Ian Heaps, joint runner-up.

Mighty Kevin Ashurst, the genial giant from Leigh, Lancs, scooped the pool in the Money Winners' table — thanks to a fantastic run during the English close season.

England international Kevin totalled £3,400 with £2,000 coming during that close season spree. An overall win in the Benson and Hedges final was worth £1,500 and he also picked up £300 for a victory in the Galloway Festival in Scotland.

But during the English season the going became progressively more difficult as the top ranks of English matchmen found themselves defeated not by the opposition but by the conditions. Few rivers fished to form and, during the most unrewarding season for more than a decade, anglers found they needed the luck of the draw to guarantee a place in the frame and the money-winning stakes.

The winter freeze-up hit fixtures badly and brought fishing in some areas to a complete standstill. But before the bad weather really set in Kevin was quietly cashing in. Concentrating on pole tactics he scratched his way over the £3,000 mark, boosting his open match victories to seven before the end of the season with a score of minor placings too.

Six other anglers topped the £2,000 mark during the 1979-80 season, compared with five the previous season. But the 1979-80 table is distorted by the decision of the organisers to switch the Embassy Challenge Final from its traditional October date to May. This means that the Embassy winners, who share fishing's biggest payout, do not figure in the table.

Had they done so Embassy winner, Bryan Lakey, would surely have topped the table with his £3,000 pick-up from the match, and second placed Ivan Marks would have finished third with another £1,000 to add to his 1979-80 season's total of £1,575.

Second place in the table went to former world champion, Ian Heaps of Stockport, who broke the £2,000 mark for the second successive year. Ian totalled £2,300 with his biggest single pick-up, £250, coming in the Southern England Pole Championships in August. Two wins in the Angling Times Winter League on the Lancaster Canal added another £350, and he also picked up money on a variety of venues ranging from Ireland's River Bann to the Derwent, Trent and Warwickshire Avon.

Winning the First Division National on the Bristol Avon gauranteed Bradford's Dave Harris equal second place in the table. The National win was worth almost £2,000 to him in prize money and bets and he picked up more money thanks to a

National Champion, Dave Harris of Bradford.

series of consistent performances on venues in the North-East. His final season's tally was £2,300.

Just £200 behind was Hinckley angler, Billy Makin, now known as 'King of the Canals'. A large chunk of Billy's winnings came from canal matches with his best performance, victory in the Tavern's Arms Open on the Grand Union Canal, yielding £380.

Two anglers, Wayne Swinscoe of Nottingham and Syd Meads, snr, of Wisbech, share fifth place with £2,020 apiece. Wayne's largest single pick-up was a mere £160 — a tribute to the consistency of this young angler who improves each season.

Wayne totted up seven open-match wins and eight second placings. But he figured in the pay-out no fewer than 46 times on rivers as varied as the Trent, Great Ouse, Welland and Bristol Avon.

In contrast, the bulk of Syd Meads' winnings came from success in the close-season Ballinasloe Festival in Ireland, which provided a bumper £1,200. Other money winning performances came on his home Fen venues like the Forty Foot, Old West River and Middle Level.

The only other angler to top £2,000 was Benny Ashurst, father of Kevin. Much of Benny's winnings came from outstanding performances on the rapidly expanding Irish match circuit. He was the overall winner in the Prosperous festival and also led his team to victory in that event.

Top Birmingham angler was Clive Smith who totalled £1,900. Clive picked up a cheque for £1,000 when he won the Angling Times/Ladbrokes Super Match in August and added to that total with wins and placings on the Warwickshire Avon and Severn.

Although no angler managed to emulate Ivan Marks's tremendous performance the previous season, when he topped the table with £7,000, more anglers than ever before topped the £1,000 mark. Nearly 50 anglers figure in the list — ample proof that more and more money is slowly flowing in to the open match circuit.

Any angler who managed to cover the cost of competing on the circuit last season certainly deserves the cash he pocketed. The appalling weather and general poor form of our major match rivers during that season was yet another handicap for the top matchmen to overcome.

Top Money Winners

1	Kevin Ashurst, Leigh	£3,400
2	Ian Heaps, Stockport	£2,300
	Dave Harris, Bradford	£2,300
4	Billy Makin, Hinckley	£2,100
5	Wayne Swinscoe, Nottingham	£2,020
	Syd Meads, snr, Wisbech	£2,020
7	Benny Ashurst, Leigh	£2,000
8	Clive Smith, Birmingham	£1,900
9	Ade Scutt, Herts	£1,853
10	Johnny McCarthy, Croydon	£1,850
11	Don Slaymaker, Nottingham	£1,750
	Ray Mumford, Tonkers	£1,750
13	Kenny Collings, Dorking	£1,740
14	Mick Hiatt, Nuneaton	£1,700
	Billy Allen, Trev's Terrapins	£1,700
16	John Illingworth, Bradford	£1,680
17	Ivan Marks, Leicester	£1,575
18	John Dean, Selston	£1,550
19	Barry Rudge, Goole	£1,543
20	Paul Cope, Nottingham	£1,500
	Ray Mills, Coleshill	£1,500
22	Steve Gardener, KC Angling	£1,420
23	Keith Hobson, Barnsley	£1,346
24	Tom Pickering, Barnsley	£1,330
25	Peter Palmer, Nottingham	£1,300
	Frank Barlow, Nottingham	£1,300
27	Clem Walden, Stamford	£1,292
28	Harry Settle, Bolton	£1,260
29	Dick Clegg, Barnsley	£1,211
30	David Williams, Bolton	£1,200

Division One National

The 1979 First Division National turned into one of the most disastrous events in the history of the competition. Hundreds of anglers failed to catch a solitary fish; the winning individual weight was a mere 11lb 8oz, and sixth individual place was taken with a miserly 5lb.

The six sections on the river Cam fished well below par but their poor form was superb when compared with performance of the other six sections on the Ely Ouse. Yet the match still produced one of the closest finishes for years as Barnsley and Nottingham and District battled it out for the title.

In the end just two points separated them with Barnsley snatching their first ever title with a superb team performance. Barnsley totalled 700 points, and provided section winners in John Allerton and John Smiles.

The team's plan was simplicity itself — although it was carefully worked out after a full week of practice. Every man was to go for fish in the first 30 minutes and then concentrate on eels. The practice sessions had proved it was virtually impossible to catch eels on the leger. Instead every man floatfished an inside line on the pole.

The plan worked like a dream and only team captain, Tom Pickering, drawn in the worst section of all, K, failed to catch. Runners-up, Nottingham had only one blank on their sheet — again in section K. But despite a fine team performance could total only 698 points, frustratingly close to taking the title. No fewer than five of their team finished in the top ten in their sections.

Third place went to hotly-fancied Izaak Walton of Preston, a side always at its best when the going is hard. The Izaaks were the only other side to total more than 600 points and their 678 total was 83 clear of the fourth side, Reading.

Many of the other big team names failed to make much impact. Reigning champions, Coleshill, finished 22nd with 465 points; mighty Birmingham were eighth with 548 points and Ivan Marks' Leicester side were 39th with 401. Literally dozens of top class matchmen fished their hearts out for hardly a bite.

Individually the match was a non-starter too. Nine of the 12 sections were won with less than 3lb, including all the sections on the Ouse, once one of the best bream rivers in Eastern England. As predicted the winning individuals came from D

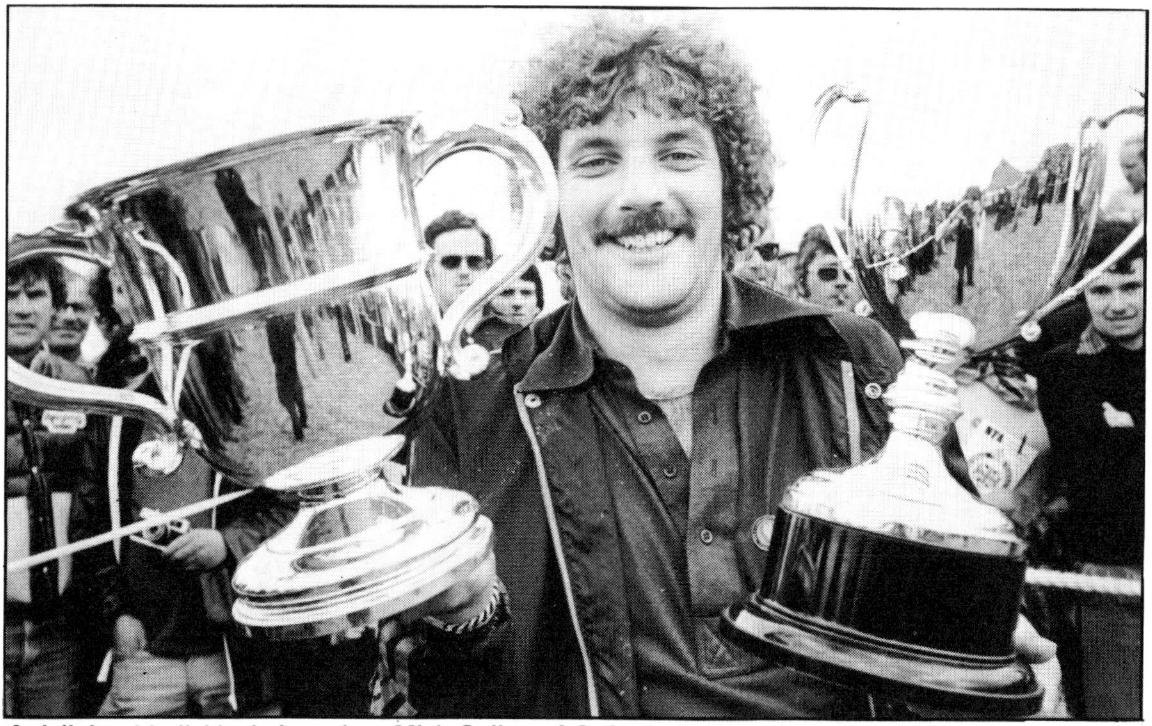

A delighted individual champion, Mick Cullen of Oxford, displays the winner's trophies.

section on the Cam, downstream of Bottisham Locks.

Happiest man on the bank was 26-year-old Mick Cullen of Oxford DAA, fishing his first-ever National. Mick fought a fish-for-fish battle with the man drawn two pegs upstream, Barrie Davies of Liverpool.

Spotting a shoal of bream moving downstream of him, Mick filled in his swim and bagged five bream in the space of half an hour as the fish moved through. His swingtipped red-worm bait also accounted for a couple of roach and three eels and at the weigh-in he totalled 11lb 8oz.

The match followed the same pattern for Barrie Davies, all the action being compressed into about half an hour as the shoal moved through. Barrie totalled 10lb 10oz and lost a foulhooked bream, that would have given him the title, as the final whistle sounded.

Third place went to the man in the middle of Mick and Barrie, Pete Thompson of Colchester, who took 7lb 15½oz of bream. The next five individual weights all came from B section in a stretch of 15 pegs between the sewer outfall and Baitsbite Lock.

Results

Teams:
1 Barnsley 700 points; 2 Nottingham and District, 698; 3 Izaak Walton, Preston, 678; 4 Reading, 595; 5 Coventry, 588; 6 Herts Fed, 565; 7 Lincoln, 558; 8 Birmingham, 548; 9 Rugby, 536; 10 Essex County, 529.

Relegated teams:
Boston; Bristol; Earl of Harrington; Kettering; Aireborough; Loughborough; Newark; Lyttleton; Bedford; Liverpool.

Individuals:
1 M Cullen, Oxford, 11lb 8oz; 2 B Davies, Liverpool, 10lb 10oz; 3 P Thompson, Colchester, 7lb 15½oz; 4 F Kilbourn, Harleston, 6lb 8oz; 5 S Haigh, Leeds, 5lb 6oz; 6 P Blood, RAF Support, 5lb 1oz; 7 M Cottle, King Heron, 4lb 13oz; 8 P Callow, Herts Fed, 4lb 10oz; 9 D Findlay, York, 4lb 8½oz; 10 T Freeman, Herts Fed, 4lb 4oz; 11 R Marshall, Scunthorpe, 4lb 3oz, 12 M Wilson, Izaak Walton, Stafford, 4lb 1oz.

Sea Fishing

by Peter Collins

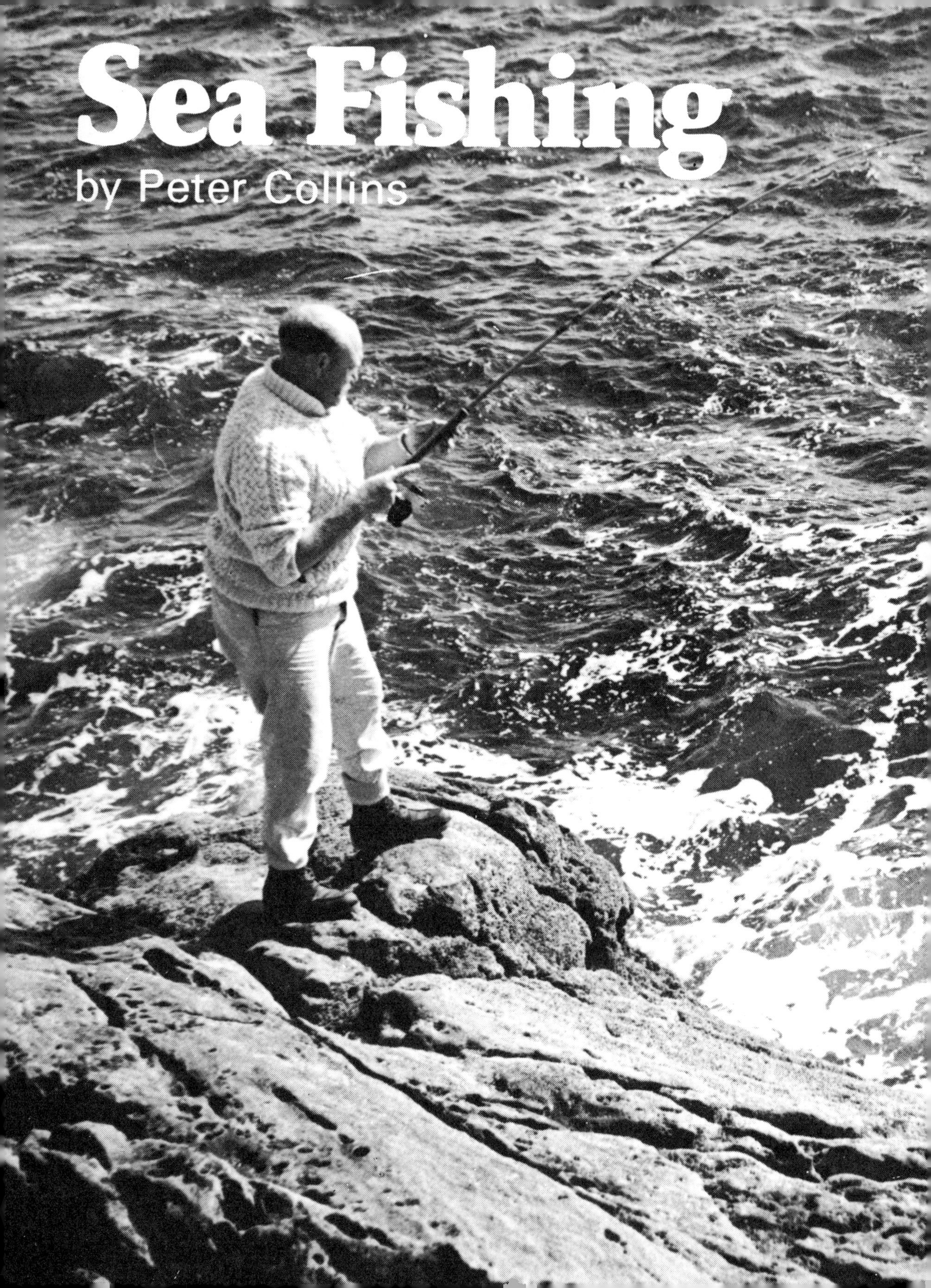

Boat Fishing

Boat fishing is the growth side of sea angling. It has doubled, perhaps trebled in ten years and the growth continues. Boat fishing is attractive for a number of good reasons. Mainly because the catch rate is better than from the shore. But there are many more opportunities at sea simply because the angler can be taken to the fish rather than have to wait for the fish to come to him.

It frequently repays its cost by substantial catches of fish that would cost £1 a pound and more to purchase for the table . . . but it is not itself cheap. The average day's boat fishing is now not less than £6 per angler but there is still no sign that there are sufficient boats to meet the demand.

Certainly weekend bookings have to be made many months ahead, with mid-weeks the only period where there is any noticeable slack. Some of the weekend pressure has been solved by boats doing double shifts — a full daytime session, 9am to 6pm, and that followed almost immediately by the arrival in port of the second party which is then taken to the grounds only vacated minutes earlier. This is, of course, easily undertaken in areas where the fish are close inshore — cod fishing off

The rewards of a successful charter boat outing. A group of happy anglers display a catch of pollack and coalfish.

the East Coast in winter, for example — but cannot be done when long hours are necessary to reach distant wrecks and reefs.

There is a continuing call for greater standards of safety at sea, with fatalities coming all too regularly. Ten lives lost in two recent accidents, one off the Norfolk coast and the other off Littlehampton, underline the fact that the demand for boat places must in no way be satisfied at the expense of safety factors. Risks can never be totally eliminated, as with mountaineering there is a risk factor which must be accepted, but there is now increasing pressure on boat skippers to provide maximum life-saving facilities on board and for the skippers to be experts at their trade.

There are an increasing number of charter boats now being operated as floating guest houses rather than as conventional day boats. They stay at sea for up to a week or even longer. In the lower section of the English Channel this has not yet happened, probably because the skippers are anxious to get the catches back to market quickly to secure the best possible prices.

There is a very thin dividing line between rod and line and commercial fishing in the down-Channel area, the anglers being regarded as a new means of catching fish. It's less arduous than long lining or trawling and provides otherwise commercial fishermen with paying customers.

It is all too easy to criticise this sort of arrangement but there's no doubt it does provide some first-class fishing for anglers who look for quantity and quality simultaneously at a time when there are very few areas where this is possible. So there is a big demand for the better-

In goes the gaff as a beaten fish is drawn to the surface.

Small they may be, but four at a time is enough to keep anyone happy!

known wreck fishing skippers and they are even more heavily booked than other men.

Another aspect of boat fishing which is showing a marked increase is via the private boatowner. More and more dinghy-fishing clubs are formed every year and many thousands of these inshore boats measuring 18ft or less put to sea every favourable day at the weekend.

The weather inevitably imposes its own restrictions on this activity but it offers rewarding fishing for all the inshore species, especially for cod, tope, plaice, rays and bass. Many holiday towns have their own slips which can be used to launch and retrieve. There are even a number of angling clubs currently employing professional boatmen to supervise members' activities.

Boat fishing tackle has never needed to be quite so refined as shore fishing gear because the fishing is generally that much simpler. The fish are, or at least swim, under the boat and are hauled out from that position.

Yet there have been some recent developments that have led to radical changes of thinking. It is now believed that in shallow water of 60ft and less fish are actually frightened away from a boat by the noise of the anglers inside it and by the action of the sea swilling against the craft.

It is suggested that in this shallow fishing it is better to cast the bait out from the boat, instead of merely dropping it over the side. So a technique known as uptide legering has been developed. This requires a rod of some 9ft, whereas the more traditional boat rod needs be only 6ft to 7ft.

The curve in the rod testifies to the power of even the smaller species of sea fish.

Many thousands of small, owner-occupied dinghies now put to sea each weekend. The number increases year by year as the sport grows in popularity.

The lead is cast up-tide and needs to settle to the bottom in that position. The line is in fact fished slack, so that a bow develops between the baited hook and the rod top. That slack helps by pulling immediately down-tide to ensure that the lead holds in the seabed. Bites usually show as a further slackening of the line as the feeding fish take the hook and then pull at and free the lead from the seabed.

This technique certainly allows anglers to cover a much greater area of seabed than they can ever hope to do by simply dropping their terminal tackle straight down to the bottom. Tangling too becomes much less — once anglers become accustomed to the technique, which has particularly proved itself in cod fishing trips in the lower North Sea.

More recently it is noticeable that more and more tackle makers are turning to longer rods. There is an increasing and desirable accent on fishing for sport rather than for an accumulation of fish and anglers expect their fish to be able to put up a worthwhile amount of resistance before being beaten.

Longer and generally softer-actioned rods are more sporting. They allow the angler to control and steer the fish more accurately and if that means fish take a little longer to beat and boat that can hardly be on the debit side.

A quite recent development has been the arrival of line class records for most sea fish species. In many ways this is a sound development since the chance to win a record adds a new dimension to the sport. The Shark Club, for example, supervises record lists for 6lb, 12lb, 20lb, 30lb, 50lb, 80lb and 130lb line classes. To claim, say, a 30lb class record an angler much catch a shark on a line which, under a prescribed test, breaks at less than 30lb. If it breaks at more than 30lb the claim is invalidated.

Perhaps the individual's decision on whether or not this is a good thing is coloured by his own circumstances. If an angler afloat in a charter boat hooks a big shark on 20lb class tackle the fish will take a long time to beat . . . which means that all the other anglers on the boat have to forego their fishing while the angler battles on with tackle which may be totally unsuited to the task.

Clearly a man fishing alone from his own boat has a better chance to fish for line class records than anglers fishing in close company. There is not, it is said, therefore equal opportunity for all.

This is clearly an adoption of the American way of fishing since they have included line class records for many years. But whether it will ever mean much to the average British sea angler is very much open to doubt.

It is apparent that sea anglers fish for a variety of reasons. A by no means inconsequential percentage is happy to fish for small fish — dabs and whiting, for example — and thus have some edible fish to take home at the end of the day. Not everyone automatically wants to locate and do battle with powerful fish. Given choice, there are few anglers who would not in fact prefer a turbot to a tope, or a plaice to a smoothhound!

Shore Fishing

Salt water fishing from the shore is more difficult than fishing from a boat. The rewards are greater in some respects though, since the successful shore angler has always the satisfaction of knowing that, by his own efforts, he put his bait in the right place. It could be argued that boat fishing, at least in its basic concept, is much easier since the baited hook is simply dropped overboard to reach the fish.

Shore anglers need a reasonable casting proficiency — how else can they reach the fish which, unlike freshwater fish, seldom swim very close to the shoreline. It figures therefore that there is a bigger proportion of shore anglers who sample sea fishing who become disappointed with their catches and subsequently give it up. A great pity, for it need never be as unrewarding as that.

Ten years ago most newcomers to shore fishing would have read that multiplier reels are a near-esssential part of their tackle. It mattered not that these are more difficult to use. They are excellent once mastered, but the apprenticeship is not over in the first beach session. In inexperienced hands, particularly when little or no guidance is available from other anglers, the multiplier reel can be a heart-breaker. Continuous tangles and the most modest of distances achieved dull even the keenest.

The answer is, of course, to use a fixed-spool reel. It's odd indeed that ten years ago most sea angling writers automatically opted for multipliers but now things have changed in quite remarkable fashion.

The British casting records for fixed spool are virtually identical, give or take a few yards, with those for the multiplier. Tangling is almost non-existent and the beginner, after a much shorter learning period, can begin to catch fish.

Part of the reason for the change has been the arrival in this country — alas we rarely make our own — of bigger and better fixed-spool reels. They have arrived from West Germany, France and the Far East and have been of generally larger diameter and have been fitted with what's known

A typical scene on one of the more popular South coast beaches. Casting proficiency is essential under these conditions if the angler wishes to be successful.

as skirted spools. This helps eliminate damage to the line within the reel itself and the sum total of the advantages have made fixed-spool reel fishing much more fashionable than it used to be.

There has not, as yet, been as much advance with sea casting rods made from carbonfibre as there has been in coarse and trout fishing. No doubt it is coming — and probably isn't far away — but at the present time fibreglass represents the greatest value for money and perhaps even a superior product.

It is very difficult to reconcile the price of over £100 for a carbon beach rod with the absolute top price of £50 for fibreglass . . . and good quality fibreglass rods usually cost much less than £50.

Experienced anglers are progressively switching to lines of fine diameter and breaking strain since this does give them the ability to cast further than with thicker lines. This is a calculated risk, of course, since fine lines need only minimal damage from abrasion to become useless.

A decade or so ago cod anglers, for instance, frequently used lines of around 20lb breaking strain or even more in sandy situations. Today good casters are using lines of less than 15lb breaking strain.

There are, of course, other advantages besides greater distance. The thinner line picks up less resistance from the tide and there is, therefore, less pressure applied to the lead weight that holds the baited hook in a fixed position on the seabed. This in turn allows anglers to use lighter leads where this is advantageous.

Fishing is a subject prone to gimmickry and from time to time all sorts of weird and wonderful claims are made for devices claimed to eliminate chance — self-striking reactors are just one of these. They catch the gullible but have no place in the sport of sea angling . . . not totally on ethical grounds but also because they are invariably ineffective anyway.

Instead of hopefully scanning the tackle shops for shortcuts to better catches newcomers and those who would like to achieve a better catch rate would do much better to join a club, a group or even an evening class where theory is discussed and taught.

The sheer pressure on the sea as a source of food — and this seems destined to increase rather than reduce — inevitably adds up to fewer fish to catch on rod and line. Conservation policies are very far from enlightened and fishing is not destined to become any easier.

So it is essential to make the best use of the best fishing tackle available, to understand the way fish feed and where they do it. A complete understanding of tackle allied to the ability to be in the right place at the right time helps to cut the odds and ensure that fish are caught.

Some of the best catches are taken in winter when conditions are at their worst.

The multiplier (top) tends to tangle on casting and has now been largely replaced by the fixed-spool reel (above).

The Big Ones

Sea angling offers a number of chances to catch really big fish from the bottom, as distinct from in midwater or nearer the surface. Sharks, for example, are generally near-surface feeders. But other big fish, halibut, common skate and conger, are almost always taken on baits fished down on the seabed.

Lots of anglers like the experience of hooking a big fish deep down on the seabed. This calls for an entirely different reaction to playing a faster-moving fish hooked only a matter of feet beneath the surface. The fish has to be hauled to the surface by an alliance of strength, stamina and the correct use of the tackle.

Of the three biggest fish in this category, the halibut is perhaps the most exciting but is unfortunately the least numerous. Its distribution is limited to the colder areas of sea around the British Isles with the best prospects in the far north, including Shetland.

We are still a long way from determining the best places available simply because halibut generally inhabit the least accessible areas of sea — either those with few ports available or areas where the sea is extra-turbulent or deep, or both. Eventually, as more becomes known it is expected that Shetland and perhaps the Hebrides will become the main areas of interest, although there are also halibut to be caught along much of the northern and western coast of Ireland.

One of the attractions of this great fish is its sheer size. It is only since the last war that the British record has topped 100lb. But in the last ten years increased angling effort in the few known and proven grounds has seen catches stepped up. The result has been that the rod and line record has jumped over the 200lb mark to 212¾lb.

The main catch ground so far has been in and around the Pentland Firth, the wild, deep waterway that separates the extreme tip of Scotland from Orkney. A relatively large proportion of the fish of 100lb and better landed have come from this area. The halibut have usually been taken on a large deadbait fished down on the bottom — a 2lb pollack or coalfish seems as good as anything.

The halibut, just like the turbot, has an expandible jaw which allows it to take seemingly large meals at a gulp without effort. In fact the actual 'take' is so fast that when watching halibut feed in tanks at the Ministry Laboratory at Lowestoft I was actually unable to see the food move or the halibut's jaws work. One moment the fish was approaching the food and a split second later it had gone and the fish's jaws were completely still.

This suggests that there is no need to delay for any length of time before striking after a halibut has taken the bait. But it is probably better to secure a deep hookhold rather than a hold in one side of the mouth where the structure is somewhat fragile and from which the hook can easily be ripped under pressure.

Halibut have a most distinctive fight once hooked. They can easily be drawn close to the boat with quite modest effort. But once they are aware of the increasing light and visibility near the surface — or perhaps it is the sight of the hull of the boat — they simply throw their tails upwards and dive at tremendous speed.

Anglers need to be aware that this is about to happen so that the fish can speed back to the bottom without excessive stress from the reel's clutch. It is an easy task to draw the fish back to the surface again — where the diving sequence is once again repeated. This may develop into a series of four, five or even six sequences of reeling in and then conceding line until the fish finally yields.

When the halibut is hooked in fast-moving tidal water, as in the Pentland Firth, it is important to keep one eye on the position of the boat. It is so easy to become preoccupied with the fish and ignore the fact that the boat has drifted several miles.

British trawlers, operating in the far north beyond Shetland and even as far as the Lofoten Islands, have sometimes netted huge halibut weighing in excess of 500lb. The ceiling weight for the species is probably somewhere between 500 and 600lb so there is every opportunity for the British record to climb some way beyond its present limit. Even so 500-pounders are unlikely in British waters . . . but we can always hope.

One of the best-known rod and line fishing areas is in Iceland where a number of halibut over 100lb and running to 150lb were caught in one particular British-based expedition. Other expeditions to the same area in July or August could have similar and perhaps even much more spectacular results.

The season for halibut in home waters seems to begin in late April with the fish apparently staying within fishing range until September before retiring to the sea floor in much deeper water for the winter. That at least is the theory. Perhaps the fish don't move away at all but stay in residence, rather like winter bass, without feeding, for very long periods.

A delighted angler displays a three-figure halibut taken off the Orkneys.

The Orkneys have long been one of the best British halibut grounds, offering a reasonable chance of success. Here a relatively small specimen is safely boated.

It is reasonable to expect to be able to catch halibut as far south as Aberdeen, or even further south in the North Sea. On the western side of the coast the fish can be expected as far south as the Isle of Man and over the entire western side of Ireland. No more than three years ago a 10 stone halibut was trawled up in the English Channel. There could, one day, be an out-of-the-blue catch to rod and line by anglers deepwater fishing for turbot or ling.

The common skate is another British heavyweight found around much of the land mass of the British Isles. Irish and British records are almost identical, on 220lb plus. Yet this is by no means the ceiling for the species and common skate 300lb near to 400lb, have been reported trawled up in northern waters.

Common skate do have much in common with halibut. They are cold water fish and frequently occupy much the same terrain. Halibut have a greater fancy for rock, whereas skate are partial to rough and muddy areas but their fishing seasons are also identical.

Alas the slow-growing common skate is another species imperilled by an over-kill. Anglers have learned the lesson the hard way and now make a point of returning virtually every skate they catch alive to the water but commercial fishermen are not as charitable. In fact Shetland, hailed as the best common skate area in the world, has been heavily long-lined for skate in recent years and many hundreds, if not thousands, of the big fish have been killed.

The flesh is inedible but is sold for fish meal at such paltry prices as £5 for a 100-pounder and if the rate of killing continues at its present level the species may be endangered in those areas where it is currently the most numerous.

The Irish have removed the common skate from their specimen fish awards contest to encourage anglers to return the skate immediately after they have been boated. British anglers have adopted much of the same practise, spurred on by the Irish example. So there is a brighter side to the common skate story and, hopefully, the species will remain available as the result of this conservation policy.

Fortunately the common skate is protected because much of the area it inhabits is still

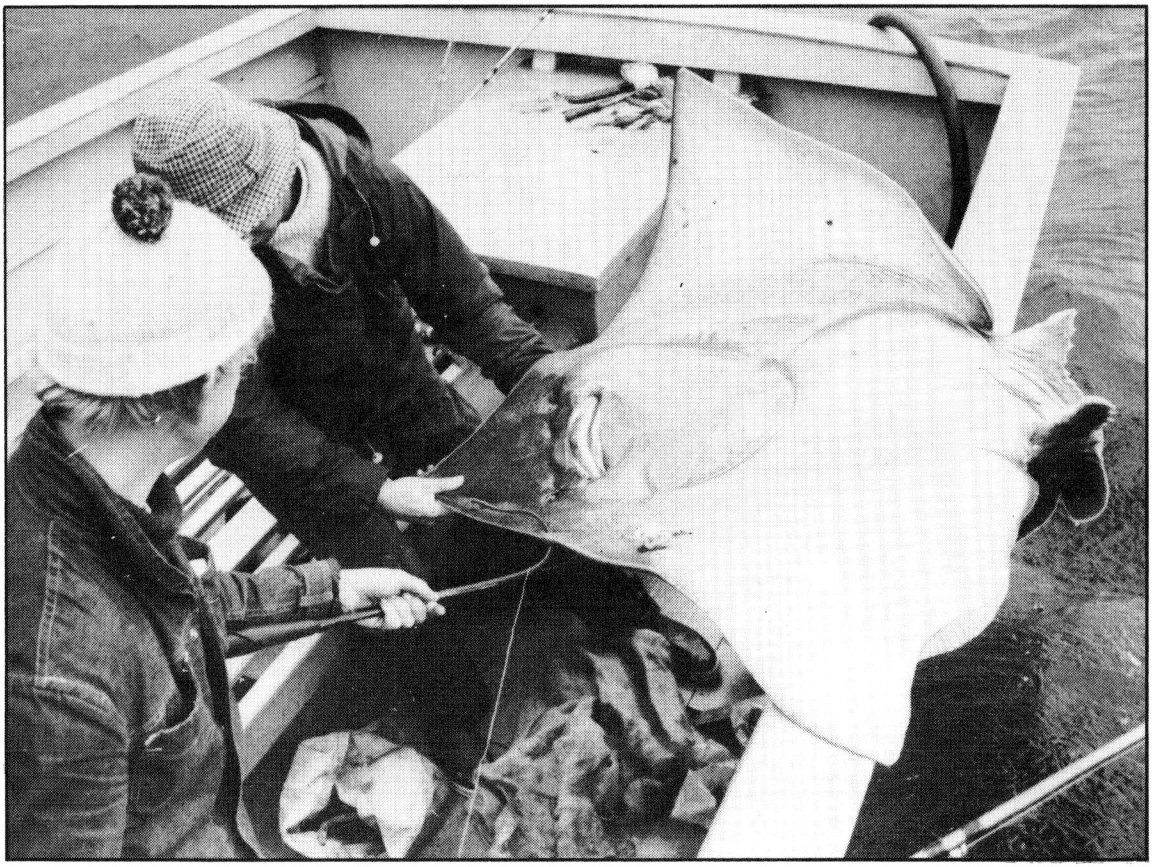

Common skate, another cold-water, deep-sea giant, often inhabit the same ground as the halibut. They too have similar, dogged, fighting qualities.

unfished by rod and line, even by trawl, because it is inaccessible. The south-western area off Ireland, for example, is deep and extremely rocky, with peaks and troughs rising and falling at close intervals over the sea-bed. This ground cannot be trawled and is unlikely to face much pressure by longlining or even by drift or tangle netting.

The limited amount of commercial fishing in this area has revealed the existence of large numbers of common skate and they must remain the nucleus of future stocks if those more accessible stocks are wiped out.

It is because of the applied conservation measures now in hand that specific figures for the big fish of the last two seasons are not available. Anglers are happy to settle for estimated weights of 'about 100lb' or 'close to 150lb' rather than kill the fish and lug it back to port for the sole purpose of weighing the corpse before it is dumped as useless.

But anglers continue to catch quantities of big commons in excess of 100lb — although it is a fact that the best results come from new, recently-discovered skate grounds rather than from areas that have been fished for many years. This, in itself, is certain proof that the skate require protection if they are to survive.

The Valentia area, off south-west Ireland, is one producing good results; so too is the area around the Isle of Mull, where boats based on Tobermory have a good record. Other favourites are Caithness and Orkney, but Shetland results are limited by the fact that few boats are available for sea angling charter work, other than during Shetland's annual common skate festival.

The Western Isles must sooner or later produce a crop of big commons and there is always the prospect of more from the sea around the Isle of Man — where common skate fishing first began. But the possibility of common skate reappearing around the Isle of Wight becomes more remote with each continued year of absence. Small, immature, commons are still reported to be present in some quantity but it is now more than 15 years since the last three-figure specimen was caught there.

The conger is the other popular deep-sea target, most of the exceptionally large conger being taken

Common skate are a slow growing species. Conservation-minded anglers now return them alive.

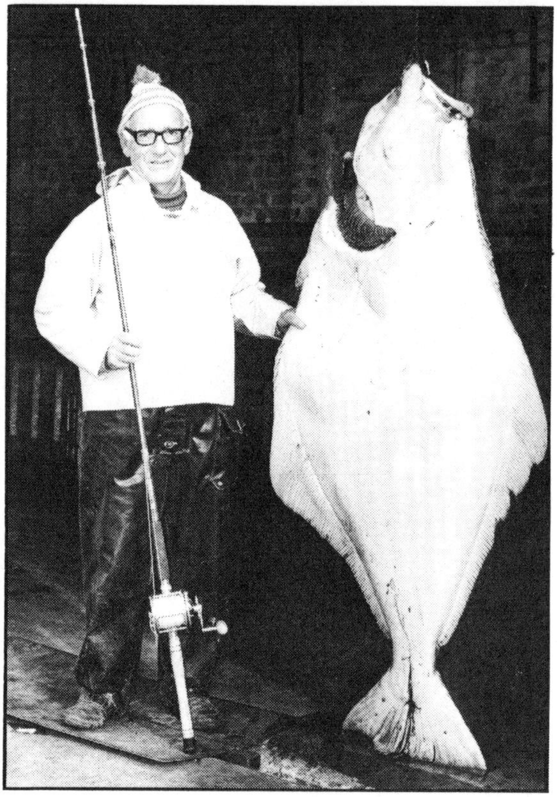

Alf Hewitt displays the British record halibut of 212lb 4oz. taken off Dunnet Head, Scotland.

from wrecks about 30-35 fathoms deep, anything from 10 to 40 miles from port. This is yet another species where rod and line results fall a long way short of the weight ceiling of the species. The best conger, on rod and line, weighed 109lb 6oz but there are known to be eels of at least 150lb all around the British shoreline. Trawlers get these big eels from time to time, mainly when they are out in open territory away from the wrecks and reefs that normally make their homes.

Such is the interest in conger fishing that is has its own specialist club, the British Conger Club, with a membership of very close to a thousand. But conger eels fishing is carried out in only limited areas. Its main ground is in the English Channel immediately opposite the ports of Weymouth, Brixham, Plymouth and Mevagissey. Conger fishing elsewhere is either never attempted or is not believed to be possible.

Yet in the bad winter of January and February 1979 a number of big conger eels were killed by the cold in shallow water. An eel of 100lb was washed ashore at Newbiggen, Northumberland, and another of 87lb came ashore in North Norfolk. Neither of these areas have ever produced any conger of note to rod and line so it must be that the sport can still be extended to other areas.

It may be that the opening up of new conger areas is essential, for some of the better-known areas are heavily fished and could be in some danger. The days of the outstanding aggregate catches of conger eels are already gone. The wreck boats that continue to obtain catches of 2,000lb of conger a day are travelling great distances to fish hitherto untouched wrecks laying far out into, and even on the French side, of the English Channel.

Oddly enough though, while the aggregate catches are sliding there remains a much better chance than ever of breaking a British record. The small and middleweight conger eels have already been taken from many wrecks simply because they were the eels that were fastest off the mark to grab anglers' baited hooks.

All wrecks will eventually restock with conger, so long as they are rested for long enough periods. But on virtually all wrecks the bulk of the really big conger eels remain intact. They are slow to move and to feed and many of the charter skippers who specialise in wreck fishing are not prepared to remain at anchor over a wreck which will not produce big aggregate catches that can be sold to the fish markets — with the boatman getting the proceeds. So conger eel fishing is, to some extent, in stalemate.

Anglers now need boatmen who are prepared to stay over a wreck, if necessary, while just one or

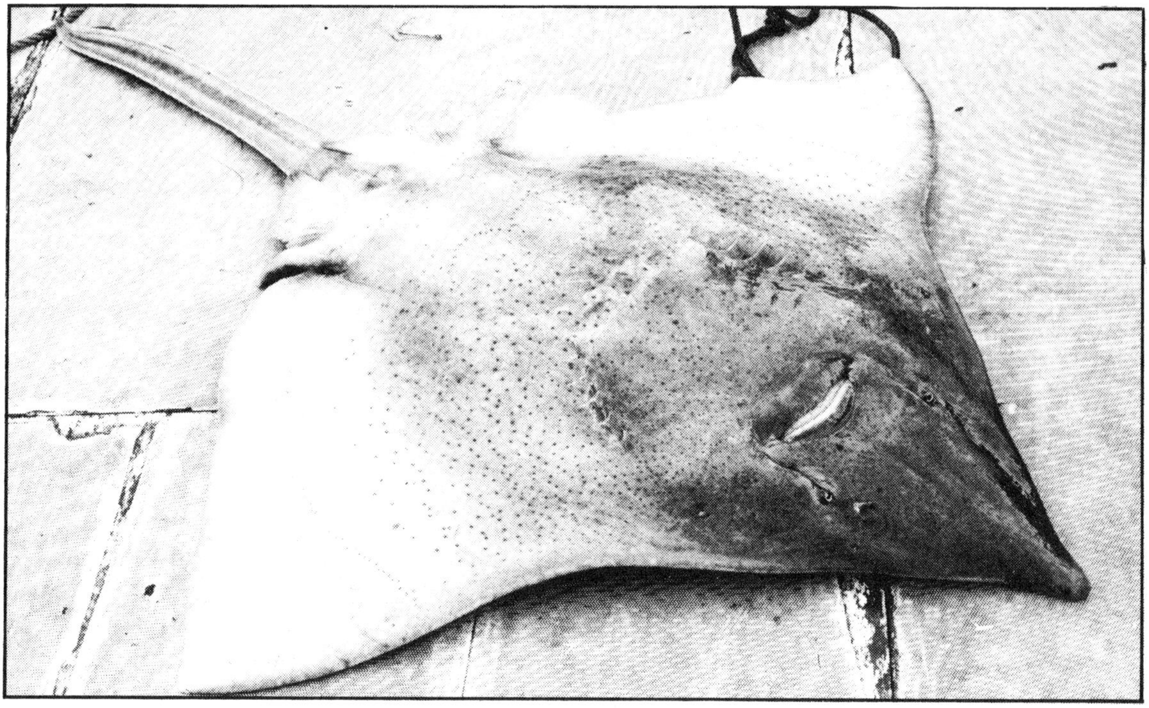

The underside of a 135lb female common skate. Angling and trawling pressure have seriously threatened the survival of the species in many top areas.

two eels are taken. These fish are more likely to be the 120 and 150-pounders believed to be in residence. The snag, of course, is money. If boatmen have to forego a cash crop they are likely to demand a much bigger hire fee as compensation and anglers who want to sit tight for a chance of a record breaker may soon have to pay as much as £15 a day for the chance.

The future rests with discovering quality conger fishing in other places so that the heavily fished areas can be rested. The main chances appear to be in the shipping lanes that in wartime led to the principal ports — Bristol, Glasgow, Liverpool and others. So long as the wrecks have not become filled with sand there is every chance that they will have stocked up with conger eels.

Falmouth and Penzance have always been thought to have great potential but this has never yet been positively established.

The offshore wrecks lay in deep water, 40 fathoms and more, which makes the fishing more difficult and tides more of a restriction. But the real snag appears to be that the ground is over-populated with ling. The rough, hard, seabed out from Falmouth and Penzance holds many ling which will always move into the wrecks just as quickly as the ling already there are hooked out. And, since ling are even faster off the mark to a baited hook than even small conger, there seems next to no chance of getting at the eels. They are, in effect, protected by the ling!

Possibilities along the Irish coast are just as good but are difficult for the same reason. The wartime southern approaches to Britain led past the Irish shoreline and there are many scores, if not hundreds, of wrecks down there waiting to be fished. But ling will again be the problem.

Even the wreck of the 'Lusitania', off the Old Head of Kinsale, rests in rocky ground where ling are extremely numerous. Every time anglers fish the wreck they catch quantities of ling but never get anywhere near the wreck's potential for conger.

Shore fishing for conger is becoming more and more popular. It is an arduous business if only because of the difficulty of reaching some of the favourite areas and because conger are best caught from the shore after dark. The best conger taken from the shore weighed 67lb, but 40-pounders are being taken annually and there must be some much bigger fish within range. The real problem is getting them ashore — and keeping them in captivity once they have been brought on to rock ledges and otherwise narrow, cramped, fishing positions. This isn't everyone's idea of quality fishing but it is now producing more eels, with the autumn the best time of the year.

The other neglected possibility is reef fishing — fishing on the natural rock formations that exist around the shoreline rather than on wrecks. There must be great opportunity for this, especially in Irish and Scottish waters.

Inshore Fish

Having read of the exciting aspects of sea angling, beginners must be excused for wondering where they can possibly make a start. Not surely, by fishing for conger, sharks or even bass. There are, fortunately, a number of relatively accessible species that are readily available. These, while requiring specialised tactics to ensure that the best sport is obtained, are at least quite gullible fish. They are unlikely to pass up a bait if they come across it during their travels.

Naturally beginners need encouragement and it doesn't matter so very much what species they catch so long as they succeed with something. The early enthusiasm is then rekindled and they move on to other things.

The species that provide this valuable service vary around the country. Along the East Coast it is the dab, the flounder and the silver eel. Further north on the eastern side it is the coalfish, the pollack and the flounder. In the West Country it is again the flounder but in the summer the silver eel, the mackerel and the garfish. And almost everywhere where the shoreline is rugged and the tide has some strength there is the wrasse, a colourful, extremely powerful fish which is very much the sea's equivalent of freshwater's tench, both in shape and in fighting power.

Anglers can specialise with all these fish and aim for quality but the smaller fish of the species come to the hook quite readily if only during certain times of the year. Many are to be found close to piers and jetties, in estuaries and close in inshore in the sea itself.

There is no real need for distance casting to make contact and they can be caught on convenient baits that are often readily available. Tackle doesn't need to be complicated or expensive. The fishing time is not absolutely crucial so beginners can, as inevitably they need to do, catch fish despite the mistakes they make.

Most novices start their fishing with simple leger tackle and therefore catch fish that live and feed on the bottom. In that category are the flatfish and the silver eels. But mackerel and garfish

Flounders are one of the most prolific of the inshore species. They favour freshwater outfalls and can be caught on a whole range of baits.

usually live in the top half of the sea and are not therefore fished for with a leger rig. For those, anglers use float tackle so that the bait is suspended in the path of the fish as they search around for food.

Other fish, coalfish and pollack are two good examples, can be caught both by offering a bait on the sea floor and in mid-water, all depends on their mood on the day.

To make choice that much easier it may be right to make the point that legering — fishing the seabed — is more successful in the winter whereas float fishing usually produces its best results in summer. It is once basic points like those are understood that the beginner eliminates long periods of inactivity and gives himself the best chance of catching something . . . it doesn't really matter quite what.

Flounders are usually located somewhere near freshwater outfalls. Could be river estuaries, or even far up those rivers well away from the sea itself. They can, of course, also be caught from open beaches but are never as numerous in such areas.

The bigger flounders leave the rivers early each year and move out to sea to spawn, returning some six weeks later. They return thin and tired and spend the next 10 months or so rebuilding their bodyweight and strength before repeating the spawning process all over again . . .

So flounders can be caught for most of the year but the really big ones, fish weighing 2lb or more, are more numerous and more readily caught in November, December and January as a general rule. Devon's river Teign is reckoned the best flounder river in Britain and it certainly continued to maintain that reputation with two 5-pounders late in 78. One fish weighed 5lb 2½oz, the other 5lb 2oz and they were the best flounders to be caught for some years.

These big fish are usually taken on legered crab baits but so far as the beginner is concerned flounders will always show an appetite for lugworm and ragworm. Once the bait is located

Inshore pollack may not grow large, but they have plenty to offer in sporting terms.

This garfish may be only small. But it's certainly made this young angler happy.

the flounder will often suck it into its mouth without giving much indication of what is happening. Fortunately the fish will swallow the whole bait and virtually hook itself if left to it. So, provided the beginner gives a flounder ample time to take the bait, there is little chance of the fish being missed.

The same is true of silver eels. Those become active every year in May and June, then show less activity through the summer but resume full activity in September and October. Eels are by no means popular with everyone. They are generally small, weighing 2lb or less, but they are quite easy to catch by fishing in and close to estuaries and harbours. Like flounders, they are caught in greatest quantities in areas close to points where freshwater joins the salt of the sea.

Eels are more active on ebb tides, rather than on the flood, but are prepared to show an interest in most popular baits. The favourite is peeler crab, but if this isn't available — and it often isn't — then eels can be caught on ragworm, lugworm, fresh herring or mackerel strips, even on uncooked bacon.

What we have in fact is a situation where flounders and eels can be caught on identical baits in almost identical circumstances so the beginners chances are further improved.

Dabs do not penetrate very far into freshwater. Plaice can be caught in estuaries but dabs prefer their water to be much saltier. But dabs are another obliging species. They may lack size but fish averaging 6oz or thereabouts are encouragement indeed in a sea angling apprenticeship.

They probably feed more readily at low and high water, although this often depends on the peculiarities of the area being fished. They can often be taken for the duration of a flood tide, especially in the summer months.

These too are fish that will take a lug or ragworm with enthusiasm. They will also take small slivers of fish bait, at least at times, so it can again be seen that the fish are another asset to novice anglers.

There are, of course, some big dabs to be taken. The British record, for a fish that averages less than 8oz in most places, is close to 3lb. The biggest fish are located either off the West of Scotland or off South Devon and Cornwall. Big dabs of over 2lb, perhaps even better than 2½lb, can be taken from the Skerries Bank, off Dartmouth annually, and occasionally from Torbay. It has to be said though that when these big dabs are caught it is usually by anglers fishing for something else — plaice perhaps, or even turbot or bass.

Garfish and mackerel are both summer species that give good sport to youngsters and holidaymakers, often on breakwaters, harbour walls, jetties and similar promontories . . . Garfish are long, eel-like, fish that feed quite close to the surface as a rule. Light float tackle cast out as far as possible and then retrieved very slowly — so that the baited hook is drawn slowly through the water — often entices the best catches. The garfish rarely weigh more than 1lb but they make up for lack of size by an incredible display of acrobatics. They leap repeatedly in their efforts to shed the hook and altogether give a very good account of themselves.

A typical inshore catch of cod and whiting taken from a popular Kent beach.

Mackerel can be taken on many methods. They move close inshore during periods of calm, warm, weather and can even be taken from open beaches as they chase the shoals of mini-fish on which they feed. Tney often give away their presence by repeatedly striking on the surface and anglers waiting and watching and poised to react to such welcome indications are almost certain to make contact.

Mackerel can be taken on small spoons and on a variety of bait and feathers. Colour is important and anglers who are prepared to cast as many as four, even six hooks at a time can get a fish on each hook during peak activity.

Alas the mackerel is not now as numerous inshore as it used to be and there is a degree of doubt about the quality of this sort of fishing in the future. We must wait and see . . . and hope that the species is less endangered than appears the case.

Pollack and coalfish are available inshore in most Scottish and Border areas but these are not the big fish found way out deep on wreck marks or on reefs. The inshore fish are the immature ones that are steadily accumulating the weight that seems to be the qualification for them to move further out to sea. Any pollack or coalfish weighing over 4lb caught from the shore is a very good fish. The average is perhaps less than 1lb but these are game fighting fish which fall readily to lures and/or bottom fishing. They can also be taken on float-fished fish and worm baits.

Another fish which really deserves a tribute is the whiting. This is the forerunner of the cod, arriving a matter of six weeks to a month before the winter cod and staying in some strength for several weeks. Unlike cod, whiting can be caught at quite short range, 30 yards is often far enough to cast if the beach shelves steeply into relatively deep water.

It is therefore obvious that whereas the cod is, at least to some extent, a fish for the experienced angler, the whiting, because it swims at a more convenient distance, is of great use to the novice. It is by no means as fussy as the cod and, another plus point, it is much more numerous.

The whiting arrive in the early autumn as a rule, sometimes even in mid-summer, and experienced anglers can catch very big weights of these fish even though they may average as little as 8oz each. There have been instances of East Anglian anglers getting as many as 60 or more whiting in a single session.

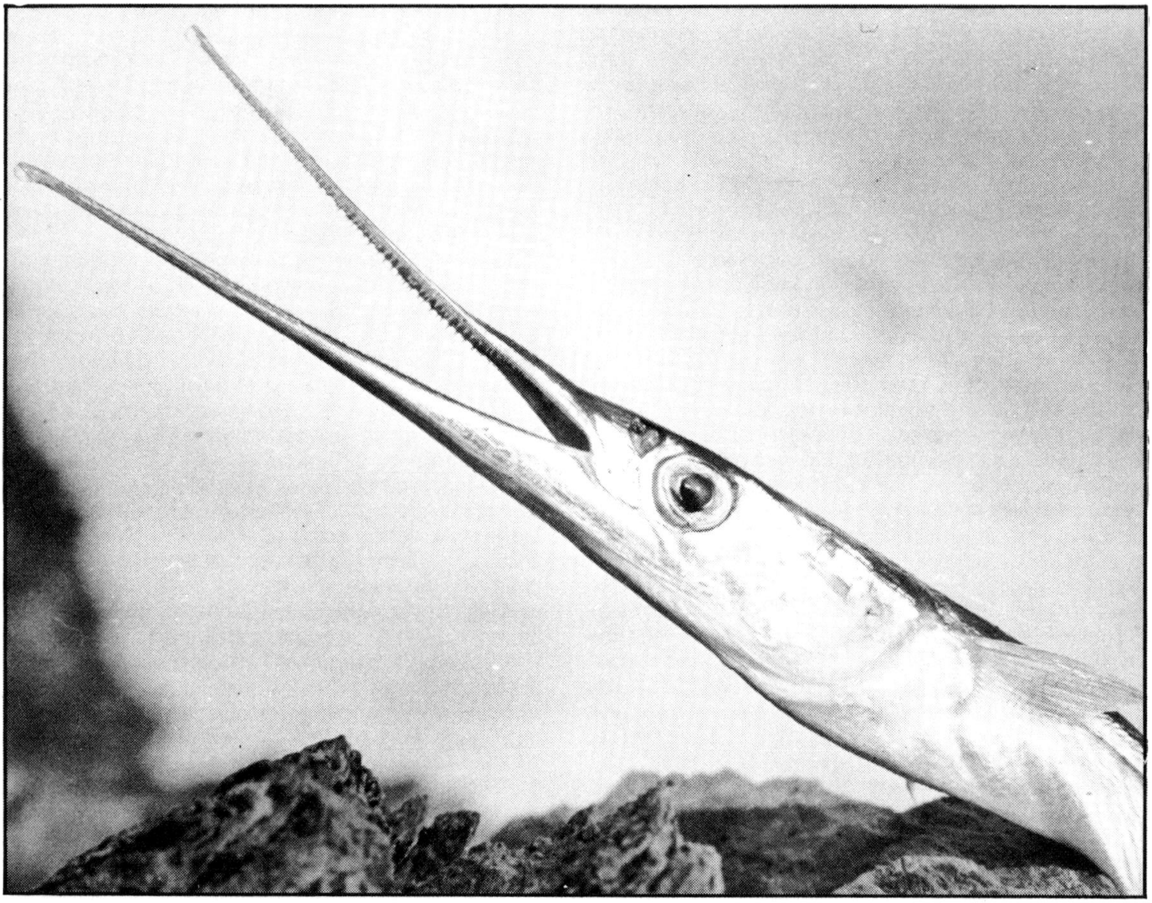

The garfish is essentially a fish of summer. It feeds close to the surface and what it lacks in weight it more than makes up in fighting spirit.

Lugworm is a good and successful bait but perhaps the best is a sliver of fish, perhaps fished in conjunction with worm as a cocktail bait. The addition of the fish very often seems to discourage the very small whiting and attract the bigger ones. An examination of the bigger catches of quality whiting made from the shore would reveal that in 75 per cent of cases these were made on fish bait rather than on worm fished solo.

When the whiting are at peak activity and strength in inshore areas 2-pounders can be taken from time to time and each autumn and winter produces the occasional fish of 3lb or better, in extreme cases extending almost to 4lb. So when the bigger whiting are running they are a popular target.

Some beaches produce their best results on ebb tides, most do best during a flood, but whiting are never as demanding as cod. When they are around in strength they can be expected at most stages of the tide. They can be fished for with light tackle since there is no need to cast, or attempt to cast 100 yards and more. Beginners can relax and take their fish easily and progressively acquire the mastery of the various techniques to the point where they are then ready to fish for cod with some chance of success.

Another widely available and useful fish is the wrasse. This is most often located in rocky areas where there is also a quite strong tide. For that reason the best wrasse fishing is from the headlands in both north and south Devon and Cornwall, Ireland and Wales. Wrasse are scarce in the North Sea where the shore profile is low and its make-up sandy.

Wrasse are another summer species. Like conger they have little resistance to severe cold but they are a shoal fish and are quite numerous in their favourite areas. They take up semi-permanent residence in their own territory and don't usually stray far away.

The more tide, broken rock and kelp the greater the stock of wrasse is likely to be. The fish are generally more active during flood tides and it is quite usual for fish of similar individual weights to show together.

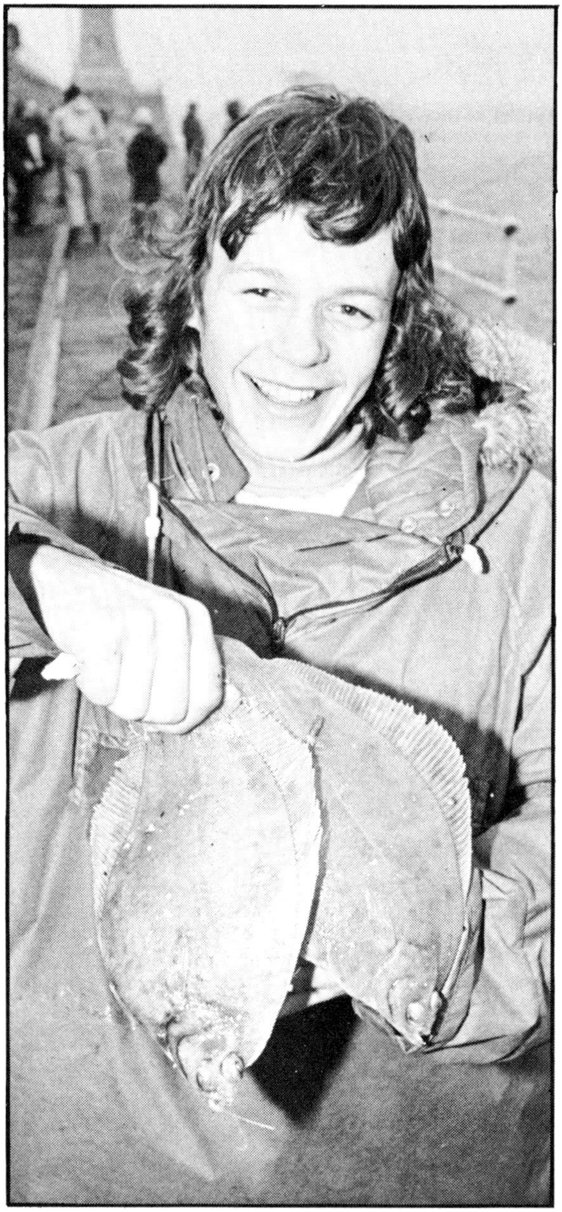

A plump brace of shore-caught flounders. The fish make tasty eating too!

Wrasse can be fished for both with float tackle and by legering — but with leger weights that are fished on weak links so that the line, hook and, hopefully, the fish can be broken out if the lead gets fast in rock crevices.

It pays to fish the bait very close to, perhaps even bouncing on the bottom, remembering all the while when float fishing to amend the depth according to the flooding or ebbing of the tide so that the bait continues to be fished at the perfect depth. Since fishing is often in depths of 20ft or more, a sliding float is essential. It should support a half-ounce bullet lead, stopped at a swivel. The line feeds through the centre of the float and it is stopped at the float top by a plastic bead and either a piece of elastic band or a nylon whisker.

Worms are an effective bait — both lug and rag do the trick, although rag is perhaps the best. Crab is reckoned the best bait for big wrasse but many good fish are taken on worms.

The fishing technique is easy to master. Long casting is not necessary, with the baited hook dropped over the rock edge and fished very close to the edge of the weed. A hooked wrasse puts up a desperate fight and must be prevented from diving headlong into the kelp — in which it would be almost certain to break the line. The fish have only limited table value and for that reason are best returned to the water to fight another day.

People who want the best of both worlds, can often retain their fish in rock pools until the day's fishing is concluded when the fish are freed.

It can be great fun learning to fish but it can also be fraught with difficulties. The lucky ones are those who either fish with a club, or with friends, or members of the family who have already attained a reasonable standard of proficiency. Anyone who wants to learn quickly with a minimum waste of their time and money is advised to explore a limited number of possibilities.

Either join a club, a group or even an angling class to learn the theories of angling as applied to your particular area. It is always difficult to learn via the written word since what applies to one area may not be true of another. There is no substitute for local knowledge gained from local people.

Tackle dealers have a vested interest in encouraging beginners to do well. They can almost all give excellent advice themselves but are frequently prevented by pressure of work during working hours. They can hardly stop and talk when the shop is full of prospective customers. Neither should they be expected to do so.

But they will advise on the address of the secretary of the nearest sea angling club — and many clubs pride themselves on their service to beginners of all ages. The better clubs have both junior sections and evening classes where the tackle requirements are carefully detailed to ensure that fishing costs no more than it must. Clubs also organise many junior events where, under strict supervision and encouragement, more knowledge is passed on.

Parents who know nothing about fishing, never having done it themselves, are advised to encourage their children to seek the help of angling clubs. Advice from that quarter prevents an enormous amount of wastage and helps ensure that the youngsters develop into keen, enthusiastic anglers.

The Predators

By a process of graduation, from shore fishing, through inshore boat fishing, many sea anglers eventually acquire the urge to get to grips with the bigger species in the seas around our shoreline... and these include species which are not resident all the year round. They come within range when the water temperature invites the fish to return.

These fish include the primary predators, the sharks, but there are some others about which there is more speculation than known fact . . .the bluefin tunny, the albecore, and others. There are four shark species most likely to be found in home waters — porbeagle, blue, thresher and mako with maybe some species, usually based in more southerly seas, showing when the temperature is extra-high.

The species just named are the ones most capable of giving sport of a standard expected in the warm seas around the globe. If they are lesser fish than sailfish, marlin and the rest, they can at least provide some classic sport if they are fished for in the right way.

In recent years it has become increasingly apparent that there are porbeagle shark to be caught around most of the British Isles. Porbeagle are not a warm water shark. They are as numerous in the area around Shetland and in the northern North Sea as they are in the English Channel. The problem with porbeagle is making an exact calculation of their whereabouts for they appear to travel long distances. If not, since there are those who claim that porbeagles are a residential species, how can their failure to show other than for very limited periods be explained?

In recent years the best porbeagle ground known to British anglers has been the North Devon and Cornish ground. Boats based on Appledore, Padstow and Newquay have taken some giant fish, including the British record fish by Jorge Potier, and others that ran it close. But these fish show either early or late in the season. Between times porbeagles also show in Cardigan Bay, off the West Wales coast, and we have yet to discover if these are the same fish seen earlier and later further south.

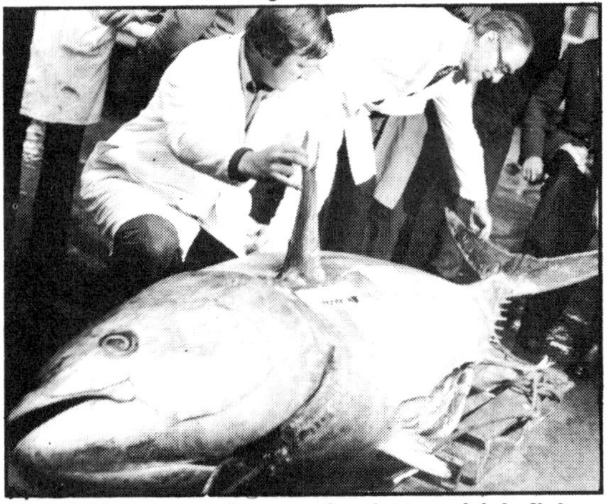

A 1,000lb tunny is examined at an Irish fish market. But rod and line prospects remain slim.

Perhaps the most surprising development came last year when anglers fishing some 11 miles out from the Norfolk coast were unaccountably parted from fish they had been catching by the action of big predators. They suspected that tope were responsible . . . but when they hooked tope and these too were bitten in half it became obvious that bigger, more powerful, fish were responsible.

No-one on the boat was equipped for shark fishing but even when the anglers used wire traces they were still smashed by fish biting through the wire.

Eventually they discovered that porbeagle sharks were responsible. They brought one fish of some 90lb to the side of the boat but would not allow the skipper to lift it into the boat. It was freed. The anglers also caught and actually landed a number of small porbeagles, fish weighing around 20lb each.

At one time anglers would have scoffed at the suggestion of the existence of shark off the Norfolk coast but although the fish contacted were small there is now the certainty that porbeagle can be contacted there from time to time. Unfortunately a shark-fishing expedition launched soon afterwards in the same area failed to locate a single shark so it seems again that the fish are highly mobile.

That is also the experience of Peter White and Erik Manson in their porbeagle-fishing forays off Shetland. They have established that, at least so far as the south-east of Shetland, below Lerwick, is concerned, the fish are only within fishing range for two to three weeks annually.

In one outstanding day in August, '78, Peter, Eric and Rea Phillips landed three huge porbeagle weighing 450lb, 404lb and 376lb respectively. They caught other smaller fish, lost more and made the comment that it was easier to catch shark than the mackerel with which to bait the hook!

On one occasion they were playing one big shark when they noticed it was accompanied by another, much bigger fish. Although weight is difficult to estimate beneath the surface these experienced anglers believe the bigger fish could have weighed close to 600lb . . . at least 100lb

The gaffs are in and a hefty shark is heaved aboard. The numbers of blue shark in British waters has declined in recent years but probeagle catches are on the increase.

more than Jorge Potier's 465-pounder which is the British best.

The 450-pounder equalled the biggest fish from the North Devon ground — that fish being taken by Rick Cotterell. The Shark Angling Club of Great Britain recorded 37 porbeagle shark weighing 100lb or more caught by its members in 1978. The actual total was much higher since only a proportion of shark anglers are club members. Nine of the shark listed weighed 200lb or better.

Unfortunately the recent past has not been as successful for most other shark species. The mako shark that used to come into the lower areas of the English Channel have, it seems, stayed away in recent years whereas at one time there was the annual landing of at least one 400-pounder.

The last real contact was by Rick Cotterell. Rick hooked a massive fish which he finally lost but that was three seasons ago. A small number of smaller mako have been landed but it does seem that the mako have changed their migratory habits. The sooner they revert back to former routes the happier British shark anglers will be.

It is a sad story with blue shark. These used to be the mainstay of British sharking but it is apparent that these fish do not now come into our waters in anything like the strength of previous years. The Shark Club, for example, records the capture of only two blues of 100lb or more by its members in 1978 . . . a most remarkable slump which defies accurate analysis.

It is a further disappointing commentary that Irish blues are also less numerous than they used to be so that the British record fish, 218lb by N Sutcliffe, fishing out of Looe in 1959, seems destined to reign for many years to come. Yet a revival can come quickly if the slump is for reasons other than a reduction in shark stocks. So there is no reason for excessive despondency.

The fourth species, the thresher, has never been very numerous in British waters. It usually shows in greatest numbers in the sea around the Isle of Wight where it is likely there is a 'dropping ground where the females give birth.

There has been a mini-revival by threshers in the last two years and this reached its climax in 1978 when J Aris beat a 295-pounder in Isle of Wight waters. Threshers are not found all around the British Isles. Like the mako they do not come to us in quantity but they are an exciting prospect. Their mammoth tail — extending to one-third of their overall length — makes the thresher a most distinctive fish.

We can never be quite sure of all the big fish possibilities that may exist, if only from time to time, around our shores. But there are known to be occasional bluefin tunny both in the North Sea and elsewhere. These big fish look almost exactly like deep-bodied mackerel and they fight very well indeed. Their numbers were sharply reduced by a number of disasters, mainly by over-fishing by Norwegians and Danes in the North Sea and also because one big migration of the fish was caught in Russian waters during severe weather and many fish perished.

Just occasionally British trawlers land bluefin tunny caught around our coast and they have also been spotted recently off the south-west tip of Ireland so they remain a sporting possibility. But it has to be said that their numbers must be very limited and the prospects of success for an expedition specifically mounted to catch tunny are slim in the extreme.

Nostalgia lingers though and it is a distinct possibility that some anglers will have a go. I wish them luck . . . but I don't fancy their prospects sufficiently to want to accompany them!

There are other occasional visitors that reach our inshore waters at times when the water temperature is unusually high. The albecore is one such species but, as with the tunny, the chances of ever locating these fish during a rod and line fishing trip are minimal. It is always possible that once the actual migratory routes are firmly established that these fish will be contacted but this can be discounted in the immediate future.

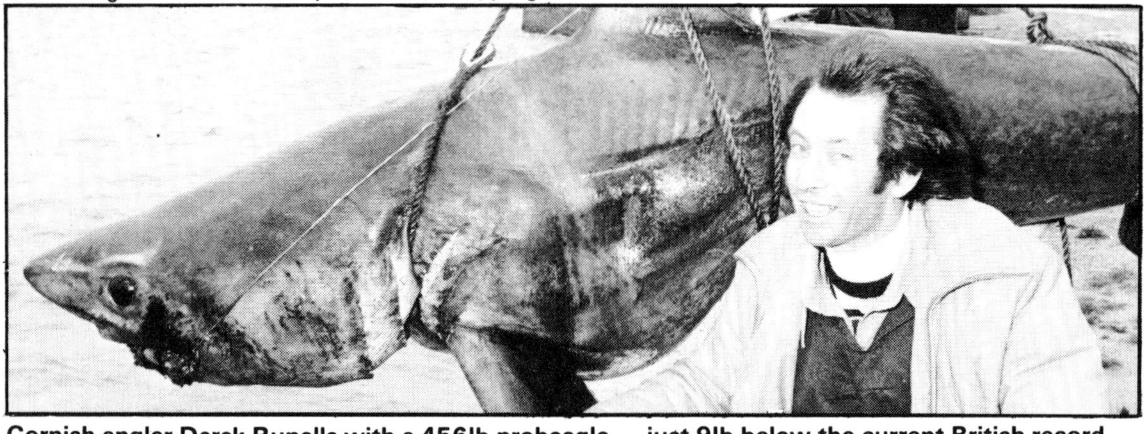

Cornish angler Derek Runalls with a 456lb probeagle — just 9lb below the current British record.

The Mainstay

SHORE

A delighted angler beaches a plump cod.

If there is a single species that, because of the quality of the sport it gives and its numbers and wide availability, can be regarded as THE most important to sea anglers, that fish has got to be the cod.

It is found virtually all around the British Isles, it is obliging, it is edible, it grows to above average size, it can be caught from boat and shore alike . . . and it gives most of its sport during the colder months when the drop in temperature has made many other species desert our waters. To add to its virtues, it can be caught in a number of ways, on a variety of baits and lures and is the one irreplaceable species should we ever lose it.

Yet it is strangely unfashionable. There's a specialist club devoted to bass, another for mullet, one on tope, shark, conger . . . but nothing on the most important species of them all. Perhaps its name doesn't do it justice.

Yet throughout the winter many thousands of anglers fish for little or nothing else and some of the better, more productive shore-spots are an unending line of anglers, night and day, over every weekend. Unfortunately anglers have to share the cod with the commercial fishermen and for that and other reasons the cod stocks are never stable. They rise and fall year by year, dependant mainly on the strength of successive spawning years.

It wasn't until the mid-1960s that cod fishing really made its greatest impact. Good brood years produced a mammoth upsurge of cod stocks in home waters and rod and line results were quite spectacular. That high level has not been maintained but, even so, cod sport has been at a generally higher level than was evident in earlier years.

The 1978-79 season was a mixture of good and bad. The stocks ought to have been better than they were, the fish tended to concentrate into some areas, leaving other places devoid of fish and results were spasmodic. Numbers of 20-pounders were taken from the shore in South Wales, Kircudbrightshire, Northumberland and Durham, East Anglia, Kent and Sussex. Boat fishing produced some really big fish — three over 40lb, best 46lb — with the South Coast area producing the big fellows.

Yet the main sport for the year came from quite small fish, cod weighing from 1lb upwards to no better than 7lb. Double figure fish were scarce and the smaller ones weren't evenly distributed.

Every passing year sees each brood year considerably reduced. It is doubtful if many more than 20 per cent of the cod live long enough to move into the next age group so the stock obviously greatly depends on a succession of good breeding years. Indications were, alas, that the more recent hatches have not been as prolific as we might have wished.

The spring run of codling along the East Coast almost invariably gives a sound indication of the coming season's potential. And there were some, but nevertheless relatively few, mini-cod to show. Impatient cod anglers sometimes become annoyed by a succession of tiny fish that pinch baits intended for bigger fish. No-one should ever regret this abundance when it shows for it is the virtual guarantee of continuing cod fishing of quality for years to come.

Cod are not fussy fish. They will eat the most commonplace of baits, the lugworm, with relish and only in the closing weeks of each year does peeler crab have any real merit in relation to its cost and the difficulty of getting it.

Cod are generally found at a greater distance offshore than whiting, but anglers who can pitch a bait a genuine 80 yards are in with a chance of fish on the right stages of the tide. Realise that some beaches fish best when the tide is flooding, others when it is ebbing, so that amount of local knowledge is vital for best results.

The ability to cast well is worth acquiring since it almost certainly puts extra cod into the angler's catch. Men who can put a bait 120 yards out will be able to take fish on those days when the fish seem, as they often do, to hang rather further out.

There's a place for heavy line in rocky situations, but where the seabed is of soft sand then lines as fine as 12lb breaking strain are superior. It is advisable to start with something rather stronger and progressively work towards a finer line as proficiency increases.

A good cod angler puts his fishing before personal comfort, so he is happy to fish through the night during the peak of the season for the extra fish that this will almost certainly provide. Cod swim closer inshore in greater numbers during most night tides, although even under the calmest of conditions fish can be taken from rocky areas where the nature of the ground gives the fish extra cover and additional feeding prospects.

Boat fishing undoubtedly produced the biggest cod catches but shore anglers must get the greatest satisfaction from their fishing.

If the cod is the mainstay of the winter fishing it is impossible to find a single species that is as important to the summer angler. But fortunately there is a big influx of incoming species, or of species that become active in summer, so there is no slackening of momentum.

Perhaps the most attractive shore fish is the bass, commonly elevated to pedestal position and certainly an attractive, hard-fighting proposition. Bass are only found in the southern half of the British Isles in sufficient numbers to justify fishing for them, but there are a number of similarities with cod.

Bass feed best at night. They will take exactly the same baits that are offered to cod and the tackle used to catch them is very similar. In general terms though bass fishing does allow the use of marginally lighter tackle, since it isn't necessary to cast quite so far, particularly after dark.

The best shore-fishing prospects for bass come when the sea is quite rough, big waves are breaking on the beaches and rolling long distances up the sand. At such times the bass actually swim on the shore-side of the breakers. They feed where the water is most turbulent, picking up crabs, worms and the like as these are exposed to them by the scouring effect of the waves.

When the sea is calm and there is no turbulence the bass know better than to look for food that is not available and they move away, probably to rocky, well-weeded areas, where food is easier to locate.

To generalise, bass run to only 50 per cent of the weight of cod. If a specimen bass is a 10-pounder, its equivalent cod weighs 20lb, but large numbers of big bass are landed every year. It would put the figure for 1978-79 as certainly not less than 300 fish over 10lb. The biggest proportion of these fish come from the Essex inshore area, fish taken boat fishing, Ireland and Wales. Each perhaps produce 30 big fish annually, with more from the West Country and along the South Coast. Big bass are not found far north in the North Sea. A 10-pounder taken boat fishing off Bacton in May, 1979, was a quite exceptional fish.

For the individual, though, bass fishing success is elusive. Perhaps this is what has induced many experienced anglers to conclude the species is in marked decline. I don't think it is (while accepting it would be grand to have twice as many as there are). The main point about successful bass fishing is to fish at the right time, when conditions are perfect. Never waste time when bassing is clearly a poor prospect. Bass are fussy to the extent that it is pointless to actually defy conditions. Better to fish for other species.

Bass will take virtually every edible bait. Rag and lugworm, fillets, even whole or just the head of a mackerel or herring, clam, soft or peeler crab, sandeels alive or dead, squid; they've all attracted very big bass.

Spinning can also produce bass. It usually brings its best rewards when attempted in strong tidal areas where the fish are likely to be close enough inshore to be within casting range. Trolling from a boat is highly effective in river estuaries and in other areas of tide where the terrain is varied to promote different tidal strengths.

Perhaps the least fished-for species in relation to its potential is the mullet. It is strong and fights exceptionally well. It isn't easy to catch but it is present in huge numbers throughout the summer months.

It is difficult to understand why the mullet should be so very much ignored. It is really a better species from the purely angling viewpoint than either cod or bass. But it doesn't eat as well and perhaps that's the answer.

The mullet has its own mythology. Lots of people seem to imagine they are impossible to catch, but anglers are slowly awakening to the fact that mullet are a great sporting species. Recent years have seen the arrival of the National Mullet Club, which has the declared intention of promoting and encouraging fishing for the species.

Mullet are a summer species. They may not migrate in winter, in fact it's a near-certainty that they don't, but the lower water temperatures of autumn kills the fish's appetite and it is believed they pass into semi-hibernation.

Some of the warm water outfalls from power stations continue to produce catches of mullet through the cold weather when sport is impossible anywhere else. In real terms, though, the mullet season is from June to the end of September and anything else is bonus, unless you live in the extreme south or Channel Isles.

Run of the mill mullet are usually quite small in relation to the ceiling weight achieved. Most of the fish indeed weigh 2½lb or less and there doesn't seem to be any real way of picking out the big ones. It's a matter of continually catching fish and hoping for the 4-pounders and better to show up.

A fine winter catch of plump codling taken during an all-night beach session. The cod is the main quarry of the winter angler.

Estuaries and harbours are the key places. The mullet there have become accustomed to man's presence and the noise and disturbance he makes. The fish are therefore very much easier to hook than the fish found in quiet tidal inlets. Groundbaiting, which is as for freshwater fish but with slow-sinking feed where possible, gets the fish interested and in the right circumstances it is possible to take quite sizeable aggregate weights.

The fishing is very positive. Most of it is done with a float so the angler must remain keyed up and alert to the fact that bites come and are gone very quickly. Mullet fishing takes you from keyed-up anticipation to hectic engagement in little more than a split second. Not that all bites are that decisive. Some mullet mess around with the bait before finally deciding to take it. So at times it is necessary to wait for a positive sinking of the float.

The biggest of mullet top 10lb, and these are very big, very powerful opponents. It is perhaps as well that the beginner is always likely to learn his mulleting on smaller fish of the species.

Boat

Boat fishing is much the more productive aspect of sea fishing. It takes anglers to the fish instead of depending on the fish swimming within casting range of the shore. But the sea imposes its own restrictions, tide and wind together creating conditions which can make fishing either impossible or ineffective.

Winter is the most difficult period since that is when the weather is worst and very little offshore boat fishing is carried out at that time. Fortunately the cod, mainstay of winter boat fishing, is as numerous inshore as 20 miles out so fishing boats can conveniently stay well within the sight and shelter of land and suffer minimal interference.

Distant water forays, extending to as many as 40 miles offshore, are the ones that become much fewer. The combination of wind and tide make it virtually impossible to anchor a boat for most of each month and the deep water activity is mainly drift fishing for pollack and coalfish.

Both these species are at peak weight in the New Year, prior to spawning. If weather conditions allow boats to reach the best distant marks, there's always a chance of both records being broken. But in recent years neither has been seriously challenged, coalfish of 23lb to 25lb and pollack just over 20lb usually representing the best of the specimens.

This pollack and coalfish fishing is a West Country pastime. No doubt it also exists in quantity and quality both west and north of Scotland but it is little explored in those areas. So the best still

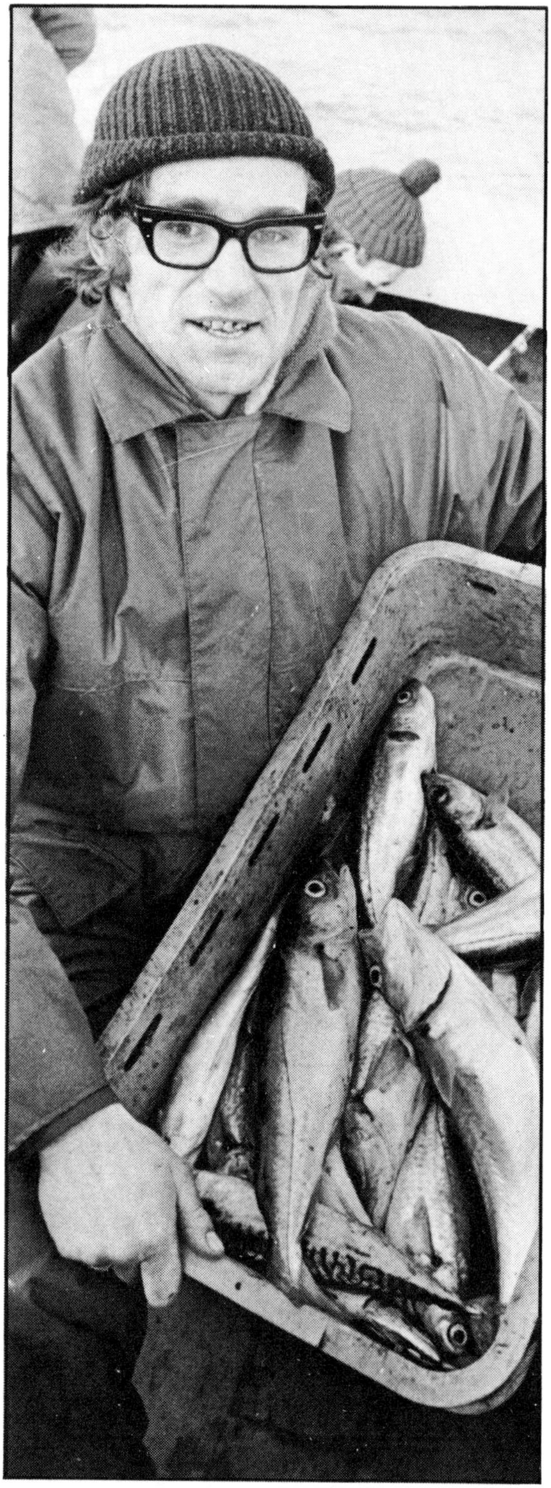

The whiting can be relied on to provide hectic sport, despite its lack of size.

remains to be discovered. But this is positive, exciting fishing, especially with relatively light tackle. Both pollack and coalfish fight every bit as well as bass, and since pollack are a most numerous species they should perhaps get a higher rating than they do.

Pollack and coalfish can be caught throughout the year, although the coallie is not now as common as it used to be.

Another attractive species, one generally found in rocky terrain, is the haddock. The haddock is primarily a bottom-feeding fish, living on crabs and the like rather than on free-swimming fish. It is common around the Scottish coast and in years of peak strength has been known to be numerous in the North Sea.

In recent years the best of the haddock fishing has been off the southern-most tip of Cornwall where the British record has been broken several times in rapid succession. The best ground is from The Manacles reef southwards in an area where trawling is impossible because of the rough seabed. Recent catches have included as many as a dozen big haddock a day, half of them likely to be fish of 10lb or better. The present record is a few ounces short of 14lb but it seems almost inevitable that this will be broken again soon and could eventually find its ceiling at 15½lb or thereabouts.

The big flatfish are always popular. Plaice, turbot and brill are all attractive sporting propositions and also make the best of eating. The latter two species are in some decline at present but plaice appear to be as numerous as ever.

The area off the Kent and Sussex shore used to be more capable plaice ground years ago than in the more recent past, but there are welcome signs of a recovery. During early 1979 numbers of big plaice showed off Deal, Eastbourne and Brighton. The Channel Islands also offer excellent prospects for these fish.

Turbot and brill are, alas, in clear decline. The Skerries, Shambles and Varne Banks all used to be prolific turbot grounds which no longer provide catches to compare with those of ten years ago, probably because of excessive trawling on and around the banks.

Scallop dredgers have also taken their toll of turbot and very big sole so that these prime flatfish have great difficulty surviving and breeding as they used to do. In the early season of 1979 a number of really big turbot, fish of 23lb to 25lb, were taken both from wreck marks, off the Skerries Bank and elsewhere along the South Coast, to reveal that the fish is still there to be caught, but the small ones are by no means common.

Wales seems to offer a much better prospect, off both west and south-west coasts. To date no one has boated a 20-pounder from Welsh water but the record for Wales is now 18½lb and continues to improve almost annually. Much of the Welsh offshore ground is untrawled so this does help the turbot's survival prospects.

The Skerries Bank, off Dartmouth, is perhaps the best known of British plaice marks, but there are others. In recent years the Scottish coast, off Wigtonshire, has been building itself a reputation both for quality and quantity and this trend seems likely to continue along much of Scotland's west coast. Plaice are in fact an attractive possibility from Cumbria northward but they are also present in large numbers along much of England's South Coast, along the South Wales shoreline and even in some sections of the inshore North Sea.

Scotland also has its share of turbot, probably east and west alike, but this is yet another facet of Scottish fishing that needs further development and knowledge before worthwhile results can be expected. Boats fishing out of Tobermory, on the Isle of Mull, catch turbot consistently through the summer. The fish are known to be in some strength off Wester Ross and commercial results suggest that the Aberdeenshire coast should also be productive once the fishing effort is made.

Brill are the turbot's fellow travellers. They run to less than half the turbot's ceiling weight and are relatively few in number. There is one well known brill bank off the Lincolnshire coast but most rod and line caught brill are landed by anglers fishing either for plaice or turbot. Again, the Channel Isles offer excellent prospects for these fish.

There is, fortunately, a real wealth of offshore sea fishing awaiting development and nowhere is there more than off the north, west and south coasts of Ireland. The east is also rich in unexploited potential but the other areas appear far more exciting.

The West Cork area, where the seabed is a vast sequence of rocky peaks and troughs, at times presenting solid rock walls up to 100ft high, has never had either commmercial or rod and line pressure. But recent explorations reveal that the troughs between the peaks contain substantial numbers of really big turbot, as well as anglerfish, plaice, rays, common skate and others. The pollack and coalfish fishing is superb in this deep-water expanse and ling are so numerous as to be a nuisance. They tend to dominate the ground at the expense of other species.

The south-west of Ireland offers an untouched potential for wreck fishing but the offshore ground is generally very deep.

Fortunately, fishing doesn't necessarily have to be in such difficult ground — although some anglers will always enjoy the challenge and earn the rewards. But there are other species found in much more convenient areas — in shallow waters and usually not so very far from the shore.

The tope can, in fact, be taken from the shore from time to time. It can be done from North Cornwall, South and North Wales and around the Isle of Skye and in Ireland but the return is small in relation to the effort required. The main requirement is a sustained spell of good calm weather conditions so that the sea becomes clear. Tope won't come close inshore if the sea is dirty, as it is during and after storms.

So boat fishing is the best prospect, and contrary to much present day thinking there are

In recent years both beach and boat angler have enjoyed good quality cod fishing. But future sport depends on good brood years to maintain the present level of stocks.

still plenty of tope to provide the sport. Cardigan Bay produces huge numbers every summer even though sport was slow starting in 1979. The cold spring and summer delayed arrival of tope from warmer areas further south. Tope migrate huge distances and most, if not all, the fish that come into the inshore waters around the British Isles move as far south as Africa during our winter.

The first tope usually show in late April or early May but in most places they had not arrived by June in 1979. Blame that on the low sea temperatures, not on any imagined shortage of tope.

Tope are another of those species that are least numerous in the North Sea. They are present in quantity along the South Coast (if not the south west), through the Bristol Channel, all around Wales and West Scotland and are also common in Irish waters.

They are powerful fish, members of the shark family, and grow to over 70lb. Fish of such size are extremely rare although a 60-pounder is taken most years. But tope have a good average size to offer. It works out at about 28lb and with the fish game and fast moving it is an exciting prospect.

Best results come from sustained feeding with fish chunks and guts. If offerings of this sort are allowed to carry down-tide for long periods the tope become interested and move uptide to eventually locate the source of the free food.

Tope runs must be allowed to develop. A tope must be allowed to move off with the bait, since in the first instance it is most likely taking the bait to an area where it can be eaten without interference from other tope in the shoal. Strike too soon and you simply yank the bait and hook out of the fish's jaw.

On the other hand, don't delay too long or the tope will be deeply hooked. Wait until the first run is completed, letting the fish take line from a free-spool, and then strike. You won't miss very many and the hooks should be quite easy to remove.

Tope are not generally reckoned to be good edible fish. There are anglers who will eat them, of course, but it is always sensible to put back everything that isn't intended for food. There's no point in killing fish simply to weigh them in and then sling them back over the side.

One most important point about tope fishing — the one which, after groundbaiting, is most likely to determine the success or failure of the day's efforts — is the quality of the bait. Fish can be caught on stinking bait . . . sometimes — but not often. The best results are made on freshly caught mackerel and the fresher the better.

Oddly enough the actual size and portion of the mackerel on offer is by no means crucial. Some very good tope anglers prefer to use the head and frame, the section that remains after the two flesh fillets have been removed. When bait is on short supply, which is likely to be the case as mackerel become even more scarce, one mackerel can be cut into five baits — four half-fillets plus the frame and head.

There are several species of ray which also provide very valued sport. These become active as early as late March in some areas and stay with us until October or thereabouts, depending on the temperature. The most common of the 11 species is the thornback, followed by the small eyed ray then the blonde ray. The remainder are much less common. They are the bottle nosed ray (a big one), the cuckoo ray and sandy ray (the two smallest species), eagle ray, electric ray, spotted ray, undulate ray and stingray.

Although hardly renowned for their fighting qualities, most rays provide a very valid extension to inshore boat fishing possibilities. The stingray is perhaps the fish with the greatest reputation, if only for the fact that in its tail it has a very nasty weapon which is both sharp and poisonous. All stingray should be handled with great care.

If the thornback is the most numerous of the species, all the others occur in isolated patches. Blonde ray, for example, show a preference for pronounced tidal areas of undulating sand, similar ground in fact to that occupied by turbot.

Thornbacks are quite scarce around the Devon and Cornish coasts, but that is where the small eyed ray is the more numerous. Undulate rays are found in isolated colonies, the biggest of these in home waters being in Tralee Bay, Ireland, and around the Channel Isles. Bottle nose and eagle rays, on the other hand, seem most numerous in the seas around the Isle of Wight. Yet the North Sea contains almost exclusively thornbacks and few of the other ray species are believed to be there.

Many other species remain. The bull huss is one that gives fair sport and good weights. It is the biggest of the dogfish and although it cannot be described, with the best will in the world, as a hard fighter, it helps to add interest to what perhaps might otherwise be dull days on some occasions. The bull huss runs comfortably into double figures and is widespread around the coast.

Monkfish and anglerfish have much in common but are two very distinct species. The monk is mainly an inshore species and is found in greatest number in Tralee and Westport Bays, in Ireland. The anglerfish generally occupies much deeper water than the monkfish and is often caught way out deep close to wrecks. That is how fish over 70lb have been taken off the West Country in recent years.

There are numerous fish that either occur spasmodically or which are caught accidentally by anglers fishing for other species at the time. There are also large numbers of what are known as mini-fish, fish that rarely if ever exceed 1lb in weight. Their appearance on record lists is purely academic since no angler who catches a record fish of any of these species can claim credit for the deed.

The Future

Excessive trawling, especially of immature fish, represents the largest single threat to the future of British rod and line fishing. Fortunately many species live in areas where trawling is virtually impossible. But the disappearance of mackerel stocks are a clearer indication of the trawling threat.

The future of rod and line sea fishing is very much bound up in negotiations, even now continuing with the EEC, as our spokesmen try to get a better deal for British fishermen. In fact their real objective ought to be to get a better deal for the fish resident in our coastal areas, for only if fish are allowed to live long enough to grow big enough to reproduce efficiently can there really be a future.

Recent cod hatches in the North Sea have been excellent but the remarkable toll taken by commercial boats of all sizes, inshore long liners (who have proliferated with the cod), and by rod and line anglers makes it all too plain that if there are a series of bad breeding years then we can be in trouble.

If the stock is allowed to sink below an as-yet undefined level it is even possible that cod stocks will be many years recovering. There is no point in being unnecessarily pessimistic — many anglers are — but the sea cannot continue to provide mammoth catches of all species year after year.

No-one has yet been able to explain satisfactorily the marked reduction in the numbers of blue and mako sharks visiting our inshore waters each summer. The decline of blue shark catches is such that only a few score are now taken annually whereas the catches often exceeded 5,000 in the better summers.

Shark anglers are belatedly reproaching themselves for failure to apply conservation measures in earlier years. They now at least partially blame themselves. A guilty conscience won't bring dead fish back to life but it must nevertheless be said that the scale of British shark fishing was always extremely modest, certainly when related to the shark stocks of the Atlantic as a whole.

It may well yet prove that a number of factors are responsible. A change of habit by the blue sharks, less desirable water temperatures close to Britain, the long-term activities of commercial long liners from Japan and Korea (they fish the central and southern Atlantic in great strength) can all have affected the issue.

Fish too are like birds. They do not have a continuing succession of outstanding breeding years. These vary between excellent and abysmal and this must of course show in the quality of the sport we get.

In the very long term it is obvious that man must eventually farm the sea in much the same way that he currently farms the land. When fish are having difficulty in sustaining their numbers they will have to be aided by artificial means.

The greatest losses occur when fish are tiny and it can be argued that once fish pass a minimum size they are at least freed from much predation and then have a much better chance of growing on to maturity. So once man can develop the facility to breed some popular species in captivity, feed them in situ and release them in due course stocks will be assured.

For the time being we depend on the fishes' natural ability to reproduce and survive in an environment where this is being made more difficult by man's many activities. Intensive scallop dredging is ploughing the seabed in many areas and having an incalculable effect on the food fish need to survive.

In many areas there are no causes for concern. Whiting are as numerous as ever and if these are small and generally weigh less than a couple of pounds, they are at least numerous, available and popular. Cod appear to be becoming less numerous, but there are more tope than most anglers will believe and quite vast quantities of plaice that anglers never quite seem able to get to grips with.

There is no real evidence to suggest that bass are being wiped out, far from it in fact, and if turbot and common skate have both taken some hammer — the former by trawlers, the second by trawlers and rod and line — there remain plenty of fish to fish for.

The pollack seems a remarkably able species. It exists in huge numbers around many areas of the coast but its cousin, the coalfish, does appear rather less numerous than ten years ago.

Ling are as prolific as ever on the ground they favour — rock and reef — and although conger have also taken a lot of pressure in limited areas there are huge untapped reserves of these fish which have as yet faced no angling effort whatsoever.

The stock situation, so far as it affects rays, is varied around the country. Probably the best of the ray fishing is off West Wales, where thornbacks are extremely numerous. Similar concentrations but in much smaller area are sometimes located off the Essex shoreline and along the South Coast. There are fewer rays in the North Sea from Suffolk northward these days but, with many of the charter boats fishing this area preoccupied with the coastal belt, there remains much more to be discovered.

It is absolutely certain that the next 12 months will see more British records tumble. Among them, the ones most likely to go are porbeagle shark, conger, bass, haddock, ling, catfish, smoothhound and a number of the rays — all except thornbacks, in fact.

The best area for development must be by long range fishing from a number of ports on both the east and west coasts of Britain. So far most rod and line fishing is carried out within an eight-mile radius of the shore. As demand increases — with the anglers' ability to pay for the extra distance — a great deal of quality fishing for many species will be discovered.

Look at any map, see where the ports are and consider the possibilities. You will quickly see that to date rod and line angling is limited to little more than 10 per cent of the sea that must eventually be fished from a boat. Some of these areas are difficult, at least in winter and during periods of unfavourable conditions, but there remains a very great deal to be accomplished. We can be concerned for some species, especially the mackerel, but there are many bright spots.

British marine scientists tell us that the sea still holds tremendous stocks of mackerel and that the annual catch totals allowed by the Ministry are realistic. Rod and line anglers are not satisfied with these assurances simply because mackerel have become extremely difficult to catch even in small quantities in most areas where they were once prolific.

It is little or no consolation that the scientists are able to report millions of tons of these fish around the shoreline if the ones that anglers would normally expect to catch on rod and line have been decimated. Certainly the catch figures of small inshore mackerel-fishing boats have slumped and show a greater relationship to rod and line catches than to Ministry estimates. We may get the answer to the discrepancy in the stock estimates in the next few years — and we have no reason to be hopeful that the Ministry is right. Hordes of mackerel in the Celtic Sea are of no use to inshore fishermen of any category.

Record Fish

Species		lb	oz	dms	Date	Captor
Angler Fish	B	82	12	0	1977	K. Ponsford, off Mevagissey, Cornwall.
	S	68	2	0	1967	H. G. T. Legerton, Canvey Island.
Bass	B	18	6	0	1975	R. G. Slater, off Eddystone Reef.
	S	18	2	0	1943	F. C. Borley, Felixstowe.
Black Fish	B	3	10	8	1972	James Semple, off Heads of Ayr.
	S	2	0	0		Qualifying weight.
Bluemouth	B	3	2	8	1976	Anne Lyngholm, Loch Shell, Stornoway, Scotland.
	S	2	0	0		Qualifying weight.
Bogue	B	1	10	0	1975	D. R. Northam, Plymouth, Devon.
	S	1	15	4	1978	S. G. Torode, Pembroke, Guernsey, C.I.
Bream, Black	B	6	14	4	1977	J. A. Garlick, over wreck off Devon coast.
	S	4	14	4	1977	R. J. Holloway, off Admiralty Pier, Dover.
Bream, Gilthead	B	5	0	0	1978	A. H. Stratton-Knott, off St. Mawes, Cornwall.
	S	6	15	0	1977	H. Solomons, Salcombe Estuary, Devon.
Bream, Ray's	B	6	3	13	1978	L/Cpl. J. Holland, West of Barra Head, Scotland.
	S	7	15	12	1967	G. Walker, Crimdon Beach, Hartlepool.
Bream, Red	B	9	8	12	1974	B. H. Reynolds, off Mevagissey, Cornwall.
	S	3	0	0	1976	D. J. Berry, Alderney, C.I.
Brill	B	16	0	0	1950	A. H. Fisher, Isle of Man.
	S	5	12	4	1976	M. Freeman, Chesil Beach, Dorset.
Bull Huss	B	21	3	0	1955	J. Holmes, Looe, Cornwall.
	S	17	15	0	1977	M. Roberts, Trefusis Point, Flushing, Falmouth, Cornwall.
Catfish	B	15	12	0	1973	E. Fisher, off Filey, Yorks.
	S	12	12	8	1978	G. M. Taylor, Stonehaven, Scotland.
Coalfish	B	30	12	0	1973	A. F. Harris, Eddystone.
	S	16	8	8	1977	N. T. Randall, at Rusty Anchor, Plymouth, Devon.
Cod	B	53	0	0	1972	G. Marti, Start Point, Devon.
	S	44	8	0	1966	B. Jones, Toms Point, Barry, Glamorgan, Wales.
Comber	B	1	13	0	1977	Master B. Phillips, off Mounts Bay, Cornwall.
	S	1	0	0		Qualifying weight.
Common Skate	B	226	8	0	1970	R. S. Macpherson, Duny Voe, Shetland.
	S	150	0	0		Qualifying weight.
Conger	B	109	6	0	1976	R. W. Potter, S.E. of Eddystone.
	S	67	1	0	1967	A. W. Lander, at Natural Arch Rock End, Torquay.
Dab	B	2	12	4	1975	R. Islip, Gairloch, Wester Ross, Scotland.
	S	2	9	8	1936	M. L. Watts, Port Talbot, Glamorgan, Wales.
Dogfish, Black-mouthed	B	2	13	8	1977	J. H. Anderson, N.W. Poll Point, Loch Fyne, Scotland.
	S	1	0	0		Qualifying weight.
Dogfish, Lesser Spotted	B	4	1	13	1976	B. J. Solomon, off Newquay, Cornwall.
	S	4	8	0	1969	J. Beattie, off Ayr Pier, Scotland.
Flounder	B	5	11	8	1956	A. G. L. Cobbledick, Fowey, Cornwall.
	S	4	7	0	1976	M. King. off Seaford Beach, Nr. Newhaven.
Forkbeard, Greater	B	4	11	4	1969	Miss M. Woodgate, Falmouth Bay, Cornwall.
	S	2	0	0		Qualifying weight.
Garfish	B	2	13	14	1971	S. Claeskens, off Newton Ferrers, Devon.
	S	2	8	0	1977	S. Lester, at Pembroke Bay, Guernsey, C.I.
Greater Weaver	B	2	4	0	1927	P. Ainslie, Brighton, Sussex.
	S	2	0	0		Qualifying weight.
Gurnard, Grey	B	2	7	0	1976	D. Swinbanks, Caliach Point, Mull, Scotland.
	S	1	8	0	1977	S. Quine, off Peel Breakwater, Isle of Man.
Gurnard, Red	B	5	0	0	1973	B. D. Critchley, 3 miles off Rhyl, Wales.
	S	2	10	11	1976	D. Johns, Helford River, Glebe Cover, Cornwall.

Record Fish

Species		lb	oz	dms	Date	Captor
Gurnard, Streaked	B	1	0	0		Qualifying weight.
	S	1	6	8	1971	H. Livingstone Smith, Loch Goil, Firth of Clyde. Scotland.
Gurnard, Yellow or	B	11	7	4	1952	C. W. King, Wallasey.
Tubfish	S	12	3	0	1976	G. J. Reynolds, Langland Bay, Wales.
Haddock	B	13	11	4	1978	G. Bones, off Falmouth, Cornwall.
	S	6	12	0	1976	G. B. Stevenson, Loch Goil, Scotland.
Haddock, Norway	B	1	13	8	1975	T. Barrett, 2 miles off Southend-on-Sea, Essex.
	S	1	3	0	1973	F. P. Fawke, Southend Pier, Essex.
Hake	B	25	5	8	1962	H. W. Steele, Belfast Lough, N. Ireland.
	S	5	0	0		Qualifying weight.
Halibut	B	212	4	0	1975	J. A. Hewitt, off Dunnet Head, Scotland.
	S	14	0	0		Qualifying weight.
Herring	B	1	1	0	1973	Brett Barden, off Bexhill-on-Sea, Sussex.
	S	1	0	0		Qualifying weight.
John Dory (St.	B	11	14	0	1977	J. Johnson, off Newhaven, E. Sussex.
Peter's Fish)	S	4	0	0		Qualifying weight.
Ling	B	57	2	8	1975	H. Solomons, off Mevagissey, Cornwall.
	S	15	5	11	1976	P. Sanders, Porthleven Beach, Cornwall.
Lumpsucker	B	6	3	4	1968	F. Harrison, Redcar, North Yorkshire.
	S	14	3	0	1970	W. J. Burgess, off Felixstowe Beach, Suffolk.
Mackerel	B	5	6	8	1969	S. Beasley, North of Eddystone Light.
	S	4	0	8	1952	Sqd. Ldr. P. Porter, Breakwater, Peel.
Megrim	B	3	12	8	1973	Master Paul Christie, Loch Gairloch, Scotland.
	S	2	0	0		Qualifying weight.
Monkfish	B	66	0	0	1965	C. G. Chalk, Shoreham-by-Sea, Sussex.
	S	50	0	0	1974	R. S. Brown, Monknash Beach, Wales.
Mullet, Golden Grey	B	1	9	15	1978	B. R. Morin, off east coast of Jersey, C.I.
	S	2	10	0	1976	R. J. Hopkins, Burry Port, Nr. Llanelli, Wales.
Mullet, Red	B	3	8	0		Qualifying weight.
	S	3	10	0	1967	J. E. Martel, Guernsey, C.I.
Mullet, Thick-lipped	B	10	1	0	1952	P. C. Libby, Portland, Dorset.
	S	10	0	12	1978	R. Gifford, Lagoon Leys, Aberthaw.
Mullet, Thin-lipped	B	4	0	0		Qualifying weight.
	S	5	11	0	1975	D. E. Knowles, River Rother, Sussex.
Opah	B	128	0	0	1973	A. R. Blewitt, Mounts Bay, Penzance, Cornwall.
	S	40	0	0		Qualifying weight.
Pelamid	B	8	13	4	1969	J. Parnell, Torbay, Devon.
	S	4	0	0		Qualifying weight.
Perch, Dusky	B	28	0	0	1973	D. Cope, off Durlston Head, Dorset.
	S	14	0	0		Qualifying weight.
Plaice	B	10	3	8	1974	Master H. Gardiner, Longa Sound, Scotland.
	S	8	1	4	1976	Master N. Mills, East Point, Southend Pier, Essex.
Pollack	B	25	0	0	1972	R. J. Hosking, off Eddystone Light.
	S	16	0	0	1977	B. Raybould, at Portland Bill, Dorset.
Pouting	B	5	8	0	1969	R. S. Armstrong, off Berry Head.
	S	3	4	0	1978	P. T. Weekes, off Dover Breakwater, Kent.
Ray, Blonde	B	37	12	0	1973	H. T. Pout, off Start Point, Devon.
	S	25	4	0	1975	S. B. Sangan, Greve de Lecq Pier, Jersey, C.I.
Ray, Bottle-nosed	B	76	0	0	1970	R. Bulpitt, off The Needles, Isle of Wight.
	S	30	0	0		Qualifying weight.
Ray, Cuckoo	B	5	11	0	1975	V. Morrison, off the Causeway Coast, N. Ireland.
	S	4	8	0		Qualifying weight.
Ray, Eagle	B	52	8	0	1972	R. J. Smith, off Nab Tower, Isle of Wight.
	S	25	0	0		Qualifying weight.

This 82lb opah was no record breaker. But it was a rare catch in British waters.

Record Fish

Species		lb	oz	dms	Date	Captor
Ray, Electric	B	96	1	0	1975	N. J. Cowley, off Dodman Point, Cornwall.
	S	47	8	0	1971	R. J. F. Pearce, from Long Quarry, Torquay.
Ray, Sandy	B	4	0	0		Qualifying weight.
	S	4	0	0		Qualifying weight.
Ray, Small-eyed	B	16	4	0	1973	H. T. Pout, Salcombe, Devon.
	S	13	8	15	1976	A. Jones, off Trevose Head, Cornwall.
Ray, Spotted	B	6	3	4	1977	P. J. England, off Caliach Point, Isle of Mull, Scotland.
	S	7	12	0	1977	P. R. Dower, in Stoke Beach area, Plymouth, Devon.
Ray, Sting	B	59	0	0	1952	J. M. Buckley, Clacton, Essex.
	S	51	4	0	1975	A. L. Stevens, Sowley Beach, Hampshire.
Ray, Thornback	B	38	0	0	1935	J. Patterson, Rustington, Sussex.
	S	19	0	0	1976	A. K. Paterson, Mull of Galloway, Scotland.
Ray, Undulate	B	19	6	13	1970	L. R. Le Page, Herm, C.I.
	S	10	10	4	1968	G. S. Robert, Port Soif Bay, Guernsey.
Rockling, Three-bearded	B	3	2	0	1976	N. Docksey, off Portland Breakwater, Dorset.
	S	2	14	8	1976	N. S. Burt, from a cliff at Portland, Dorset.
Rockling, Shore	B	1	0	0		Qualifying weight.
	S	1	1	4	1976	A. Bayes, Gristhorpe, Nr. Scarborough, Yorks.
Salmon, Coho	MINIMUM QUALIFYING WEIGHT TO BE FINALISED FOR BOAT RECORD.					
	S	1	8	1	1977	R. J. McCracken, St. Sampsons, Guernsey, C.I.
Sea Scorpion, Short-spined	B	2	3	0	1973	R. Stephenson, Grt. Cumbrae Island, Scotland.
	S	2	2	8	1972	R. W. Tarn, off Roker South Pier, Sunderland.
Scad (Horse Mackerel)	B	3	5	3	1978	M. A. Atkins, at Torbay, Devon.
	S	2	5	13	1977	W. K. Rail, at North Cliffs, Cornwall.
Shad, Allis	B	3	0	0		Qualifying weight.
	S	4	12	7	1977	P. B. Gerrard, off Chesil Beach, Dorset.
Shad, Twaite	B	3	2	0	1949	T. Hayward, Deal, Kent.
	B	3	2	0	1954	S. Jenkins, Torbay, Devon.
	S	2	12	0	1978	J. W. Martin, at Garlieston, Wigtownshire, S.W. Scotland.
Shark, Blue	B	218	0	0	1959	N. Sutcliffe, Looe, Cornwall.
	S	75	0	0		Qualifying weight.
Shark, Mako	B	500	0	0	1971	Mrs. J. M. Yallop, off Eddystone Light.
	S	75	0	0		Qualifying weight.
Shark, Porbeagle	B	465	0	0	1976	J. Potier, off Padstow, Cornwall.
	S	75	0	0		Qualifying weight.
Shark, Six-gilled	B	9	8	0	1976	F. E. Beeton, south of Penlee Point, Plymouth, Devon.
	S	NO MINIMUM QUALIFYING WEIGHT.				
Shark, Thresher	B	295	0	0	1978	H. J. Aris, at Dunose Head, south of Isle of Wight.
	S	75	0	0		Qualifying weight.
Smoothhound, Starry	B	20	15	12	1978	B. J. Allpress, at Bradwell-on-Sea, Essex.
	S	23	2	0	1972	D. Carpenter, Beach at Bradwell-on-Sea, Essex.
Smoothhound	B	28	0	0	1969	A. T. Chilvers, Heacham, Norfolk.
	S	14	14	12	1977	A. J. Peacock, at St. Donats, Glamorgan, Wales.
Sole	B	4	0	0		Qualifying weight.
	S	4	8	0	1978	H. C. L. Pike, at Platte Saline Beach, Alderney, C.I.
Sole, Lemon	B	2	2	0	1976	J. Gordon, at Loch Goil Head, off Loch Long, Firth of Clyde, Scotland.
	S	2	2	15	1971	D. R. Duke, Victoria Pier, Douglas, Isle of Man.
Spanish Mackerel	B	1	0	6	1972	P. Jones, off Guernsey, C.I.
	S	1	0	0		Qualifying weight.
Spurdog	B	21	3	7	1977	P. R. Barrett, off Porthleven, Cornwall.
	S	16	12	8	1964	R. Legg, Chesil Beach, Dorset.
Sunfish	B	108	0	0	1976	T. F. Sisson, off Saundersfoot, Wales.
	S	49	4	0	1976	M. G. H. Merry, Fisherman's Cove, Cornwall.

Species		lb	oz	dms	Date	Captor
Tadpole Fish	B	1	0	0		Qualifying weight.
	S	1	3	12	1977	D. A. Higgins, Browns Bay, Whitley Bay, Tyne and Wear.
Tope	B	74	11	0	1964	A. B. Harries, Caldy Island.
	S	54	4	0	1975	D. Hastings, Loch Ryan, Wigtownshire, Scotland.
Torsk	B	12	1	0	1968	D. Pottinger, Shetland.
	S	5	0	0		Qualifying weight.
Trigger Fish	B	4	9	5	1975	E. Montacute, Weymouth Bay, Dorset.
	S	4	6	0	1975	M. J. Blew, Bossington Beach, Somerset.
Tunny	B	851	0	0	1933	L. Mitchell Henry, Whitby, Yorks.
	S	100	0	0		Qualifying weight.
Turbot	B	32	3	0	1976	D. Dyer, off Plymouth, Devon.
	S	28	8	0	1973	J. D. Dorling, Dunwich Beach, East Suffolk.
Whiting	B	6	4	0	1977	S. Dearman, West Bay, Bridport, Dorset.
	S	3	2	0	1976	C. T. Kochevar, off Dungeness Beach, Kent.
Whiting, Blue	B	1	12	0	1977	J. H. Anderson, Loch Fyne, Scotland.
	S	NO MINIMUM QUALIFYING WEIGHT.				
Witch	B	1	0	0		Qualifying weight.
	S	1	2	13	1967	T. J. Barathy, Colwyn Bay, Wales.
Wrasse, Ballan	B	7	8	5	1975	M. B. Hale, north of Herm, C.I.
	S	8	6	6	1976	R. W. Le Page, Bordeaux Beach, Guernsey, C.I.
Wrasse, Cuckoo	B	2	0	8	1973	A. M. Foley, off Plymouth, Devon.
	S	1	4	8	1973	R. Newton, Holyhead Breakwater, Wales.
Wreckfish	B	7	10	0	1974	Cdr. E. St. John Holt, Looe, Cornwall.
	S	2	0	0		Qualifying weight.

Rita Barrett with her 6lb 3oz 3dr whiting which held the record until 1977.

Trout Fishing

by Clive Nash

Trout Fishing

Judging by the way it started, 1979 looks like going down as the year the rainbow trout WASN'T broken. True, some cracking fish were taken during the first part of the year, and some of them came from very unexpected waters, but Avington and its imitators surprised everyone by staying out of the rainbow limelight.

And anyone who thinks that is simply because fish farmers like Sam Holland have reached their upper limits in producing "supertrout" is only showing how really naive he is about the modern stillwater trouting scene.

No; the simple truth was that the publicity value of jumbo rainbows had lost its strength. Hardened reporters hardly stirred an eyelid as double figure fish were reported. Let's face it. They are nothing new, and have been turning up in so-called 'wild' Welsh waters.

Even the anglers reporting the huge catches seemed relatively unawed by their feat. Monthly rainbow record breakers went by the board quite simply because Sam Holland and his contemporaries had a new toy to play with — the brookie.

The American brook trout has been known in Britain for many years now, and restricted local populations have been thriving in certain out-of-the-way locations. It fed greedily in even the most dreaded conditions, fought quite well, and ate well — but it was small.

No-one got excited at catching fish around the pound, at least not after several years of concentrated jumbo rainbow promotion. Then some people discovered that the humble brookie would survive in conditions that would almost wipe out the coddled stew-fed rainbow and even gave the arrogant wild brownie a hard time.

Some Welsh waters received small, experimental, stockings, but down in Cornwall and Devon, the South West Water Authority really got stuck in.

Brookies, they discovered, were perfect for their bleak, acidic, moorland waters. Reservoirs that had been non-starters as fisheries suddenly became big business.

Fly fishermen with jaded palates wanted to know more about this exciting new species; they wanted to catch something different. Sam Holland, the man who gave us the now world-famous Avington "strain" of rainbows, soon jumped on the bandwaggon.

The brook trout record, that had so long been held by a fish that would have been dwarfed by the average stockie on most waters, was smashed out of existence — regularly.

It was "supertrout" time all over again. The great publicity machine at first coughed and spluttered and then roared into life with a whole new batch of propoganda.

Fisheries were made to feel inadequate if they hadn't stocked with brookies. But this time round, it wasn't an Avington-type exclusive.

Those West Country reservoirs were no slouches either, and in a matter of days had topped Sam Holland's new record three times. The venue was Fernworthy, a little known fishery near Okehampton, Devon. Little-known until then, but over the next few weeks it was destined to hang on the lips of trout men all over Britain.

But apart from the appearance of brook trout, 1979 was short on new innovations — and action. The foundations for the poor season were laid way back in 78, when the worst British winter for years started to creep in.

As the temperature dropped, the wind rose, bringing first driving rain, freezing sleet and then snow. And what snow. No-one needs reminding about the harshness of that winter.

It affected every aspect of normal life in Britain — and fishing certainly wasn't excluded. Rainbows have never been renowned for their overwintering ability, and that winter killed off fish in their thousands.

Those that did survive went deep, and stayed deep well after the season opened in early Spring. Many fisheries had problems with their stock fish for the new season. The low temperatures produced slow growth rates and a shortage of fish.

Anglers all over the country complained about smaller than usual stockies, but many fisheries could do nothing but cope. Those with their own hatchery facilities were a little better off.

But that wasn't the only problem by any means. Even by early spring, the winter showed little sign of letting up. Early openers like Packington and many of the Welsh waters saw their first fishing amid the snowstorms — and catches reflected the conditions.

Fish stayed deep and were very lethargic. Even confirmed lure pullers had little joy until May brought a little sunshine to start warming up the waters.

As the weather continued to improve, so did catches — but nowhere could be described as really great fishing. But, despite all these great difficulties, the number of anglers lining the banks of reservoirs and small fisheries alike had grown again.

In the very worst of conditions, trout fishing had again proved itself as the fastest growing branch of angling.

Cambridgeshire angler Percy Kidd with Grafham's largest brownie of 1978, taken from the dam wall on a red and white streamer lure.

Bristol Waters

The drought years of the middle 1970's have a lot to answer for in the world of trout fishing. As if it wasn't enough that the heatwaves should completely ruin sport for fly fishermen when they were actually happening, their hangover effects still plague some fisheries.

And West Country anglers, at least those who fish the Bristol Waterworks Company's complex, are suffering more than most. That searing sun laid bare acres of once fertile margins around both Chew Valley Lake and Blagdon. Then it proceeded to bake all the life out of them.

A magnificent trio of trout taken from Blagdon. Both Chew and Blagdon have suffered from a combination of drought and floods.

Weed beds, once rich in insect life, that attracted browsing trout to within easy casting distance of the shore disappeared completely.

But, with the incredible rainfall over the last winter and spring, the water levels at Chew and Blagdon rose dramatically — setting a new record level for Chew. Those scorched acres now lay under feet of water — right where bank men could cast to.

With no weed growth there was no insect life — nothing to attract the trout close to the shore. The droughts had finally completed a sort of No Man's Land which unfortunately devastated sport for bank anglers in 1979.

It was a disappointing anti-climax after the hectic finish to the previous season. Despite difficult fishing conditions which had slowed sport right down in August, 1978, the closing months had seen some fabulous sport.

No catch figures were broken, but both lakes come pretty close — especially considering the cold start and that August doldrum period.

The 1979 season couldn't have started in worse conditions — with a full blown Force Nine wind tearing across Chew and Blagdon. But hundreds of anglers had made their annual pilgrimage — many travelling from the extremes of Britain — to what are acknowledged by all trout men as the original stillwater venues.

Despite the freezing temperatures and that harsh, biting, wind, fish did show up. Despite a slow opening day, the next week or so saw 2,000 trout taken from the two waters.

Most of the fish came from boats, while bank anglers discovered the harsh reality that was to stay with them for as long as the extremely high water levels held. Ironically, though, the best fish of those early days, an 8lb 3oz Chew rainbow and a 7lb 1oz Blagdon specimen, both came from the bank.

Lures in basic black and white patterns retrieved slowly in the depths of both reservoirs provided most fish. Fly life was non-existent, so it was fish imitators all the way.

Reservoir Figures:

Blagdon

Total catch 1978	Total to June 1979	Best brown 1978	Best brown 1979	Best rainbow 1978	Best rainbow 1979
12,000	5,000	5lb 2oz	4lb 1oz	7lb 9oz	7lb 1oz

Chew Valley

Total catch 1978	Total to June 1979	Best brown 1978	Best brown 1979	Best rainbow 1978	Best rainbow 1979
14,000	7,000	5lb 7oz	6lb	8lb 12oz	8lb 3oz

Those southerly winds hit sport hard, especially at Chew, with the odd easterly providing a bit of variety in direction, but not numbers of trout. As the winds died down, though, sparse hatches of buzzers began to appear slowly at sporadic intervals.

The bank men still found life almost impossible, but boat anglers discovered a wealth of fish feeding in shallow water well offshore. The Roman Shallows at Chew were a perfect example, but anywhere shallow enough to encourage weed growth seemed to produce fish.

The lures were packed away in favour of more traditional attractors like Mallard and Claret, Silver Invicta and Peter Ross, although the Worm Fly continued to catch its share of trout.

The daytime fishing was still hard but, as the sun warmed some life into the water, Chew and Blagdon started to respond more to buzzers, Pheasant Tail Nymph and the Grenadier during those sparse evening rises. And they were late evening hatches, with fish appearing mostly after 9 pm.

By June, trout started to appear on the top more consistently, but still spread thinly over the weedy shallows. Colour began to play a more important role, with orange-based patterns like the Whisky Fly starting to pick up fish steadily.

Catches had grown from a little under a thousand a week to average well over that, touching the 2,000 mark on a number of weeks. But the bulk of fish were still falling to boat anglers. Those die-hard men were still fighting a losing battle.

They were waiting patiently, though, for their time to come. And they knew it would, as soon as the water levels dropped and they could at last cast beyond that barren No Man's Land into water that actually held some insect life and foraging trout.

Large trout and happy angler — a combination which has made Chew a magnet for anglers.

Rutland

Leicestershire's Rutland Water "superfishery" continued its amazing success story into the 1979 season, grabbing the year's limelight from opening day.

In fact, this year's success story started even before the official opening day, when Angling Times editorial manager Bob Feetham set a new rainbow record for the water with a 6lb 14oz fish on the fishery's special press preview day.

Bob fished a size 14 long shanked Black Chenille from the bank at Whitwell Creek. But Bob's success story was short lived as Rutland produced an amazing run of fish that included four rainbows over that weight, topped by an 8lb 13oz monster, and a new record 7lb 7oz brownie.

It all started on opening day, with the big brownie. Dick Spring, from Nuneaton, Warwickshire, fished a White Lure from the bank at Hambleton Peninsular to take that fish.

Within an hour the rainbow record went as well to complete a fabulous double. Mervyn Bronham had travelled overnight from his South Wales home at Morriston, Swansea, to be in at the Rutland opening.

Mervyn had booked a boat, and reckoned the money well spent after his record-breaker came to a Baby Doll fished in the reservoir's North Arm.

The turn-out for that opening day was fantastic, with 1,200 anglers from all over Britain lining the banks. In the week that followed, Rutland proved that those big fish were no flukes.

Nigel Roberts, from Sawston, Cambs, took a 7¾lb rainbow. Rotherham, Yorks, visitor Dennis Lingley went one better, with a 7lb 15oz fish.

Then Brian Thomas, from Carlton, Nottingham, became the second man to break Rutland's milestone 8lb limit with an 8lb 2oz rainbow.

But not everyone was pleased to see those fish. Anglers who had actually seen the giant-sized rainbows claimed they were just big brood fish stocked to add spice — not fish that had overwintered and grown naturally in Rutland's own waters.

The Anglian Water Authority were quick to issue a strong denial, but the damage was done. The big rainbows had been labelled as a cheap publicity gimmick, and anglers quoted the old adage — "there is no smoke without fire".

Whatever the origin of those rainbows, nobody could deny that Rutland went from strength to strength to show even better form than the halcyon two previous seasons.

What had been the high spots in 1978 became commonplace in the new season.

The 1978 season had finished with the expected record catch and attendance figures, and a group of regulars had really cashed in on some late season big brown action.

Those regulars had spent two years searching Rutland's vast acreage of water and their efforts paid dividends in terms of increased catches — and much bigger fish.

They discovered a 30 acre hotspot in the huge North Arm of the reservoir, where big brownies were packed tight. Lead core lines and giant-sized lures produced regular limits of three, four and even 5lb brown trout for the boat anglers who knew the spot.

Bank men also cashed in on the sport, taking a few decent fish from bays in both arms and in Barnsdale Creek during some amazing evening rises.

But then came that long and harsh winter. Britain was ravaged by blizzards, freezing temperatures and driving winds.

How would the fish have overwintered in those conditions, and how long would they take to come on the feed? The anglers needn't have worried. Right from the off, Rutland fished its head off.

The water level was at its highest ever, because the Anglian Water Authority were engaged in various tests to check the strength of the dam.

That high water level meant acres and acres of newly flooded land — it was just like fishing a virgin water all over again.

The bank sport was second to none as thousands of trout, hungry after the ravages of winter, moved inshore to gorge themselves on all the worms packed into those new acres of reservoir bed.

The main hotspots were around the creek and feeder streams, though nowhere along the shoreline was exactly short of fish.

Unfortunately, the majority of those fish were rainbows, still in poor condition. Lovely fish to catch in a month or so, but too black for comfort right at the start.

The other problem was that while the new waterline was packed with fish, it was also packed with newly flooded fences and bushes — perfect

Reservoir Figures:

Total catch 1978	Total to June 1979	Best brown 1978	Best brown 1979	Best rainbow 1978	Best rainbow 1979
69,217	24,917	6lb 10oz	7lb 7oz	5lb 14oz	8lb 13oz

The first of Rutland's record-breaking rainbows — Bob Feetham's 6lb 14oz fish.

snags for unwary visitors who didn't know the lie of the land.

The great sport wasn't spread all over Rutland, though, with little early action at all in the South Arm.

The North Arm, Normanton Bank and Whitwell Creek were packed with fish — though the pellet feeding of caged trout may have had something to do with the numbers of fish at Whitwell.

The boat fishing was slower to pick up, but by the end of May those fish had glutted themselves on the worms inshore and were moving outwards into deeper water for new grazing grounds.

There was a lot of fuss in November, 1978, about the stocking of several batches of eight to 10oz fish — but by the spring of 79 they had packed on weight and no-one was complaining about the bright pound-plus trout.

As the weather warmed up, fish spread out more and at last started turning up in the South Arm, for boat men at least.

Drifting with ten yards of lead core line produced a run of big browns and rainbows. The successful lure was a newly designed white and yellow tube fly.

Another of the top takers was the Baby Doll, tied in white, orange and red.

By June, the buzzers were thick and big, with many almost an inch long. Trout men tied their artificials on size 12 long shanks — almost unheard of in the past.

By mid-season, fish were plentiful, though anglers needed a little cloud cover in the middle of the day.

The evening rises were a different matter, though, and evening ticket sales soared.

One problem that did occur, and looks likely to get even bigger, was that of pike and other coarse fish. Despite extensive efforts by the Anglian Water Authority when Rutland was first flooded, coarse fish are thriving as well as, and possibly better than, at Grafham.

All the bays were packed with pike, with trout men taking fish to 8lb, even on nymphs. Vast shoals of rudd and roach in the 12oz range were spotted in many areas. In some they had even shifted the trout.

The Sailing Club Bay was a perfect example. It was fishing very well until large numbers of roach moved in.

Rainbows

by Bob Church

I have lost count of the times I have been asked for the secret recipe to consistent success in rainbow trout fishing. And I always give the same answer — boatmanship. The track records of all the top-rated trout men provide all the evidence I need to back that statement.

Many years ago, the Northampton trout anglers were consistently bringing in limit catches. So consistently, in fact, that their methods came under suspicion from other anglers.

And in those days, our behaviour didn't exactly set their minds at rest, as we "smuggled" our latest secret aids onto reservoir boats. They were home-made rudders, taken onto the boat in pieces to be assembled out of sight of prying eyes. We used them to control boat drift across the wind, and we came to call them lee-boards.

We also used home-made drogues, which easily outperformed the archaic designs offered as standard equipment on so many waters.

The advantages of these new pieces of equipment were tremendous, as our catches proved, and they set the pace for a full scale revolution in boat fishing for trout. Rainbows, especially, were suckers for the new techniques, and we learned more about boatmanship every single season.

A drogue allows you to slow the rate of drift of your boat, but you still only travel in a straight line with the wind. The lee-board enables you to tack across the wind, offering the chance to cover more ground on every drift and to use a wider range of tactics.

The simplest is to cast a fly out to the side and then let the line form a big bow in the current as you continue drifting. This draws the fly across the noses of fish feeding near the surface, and hard takes often come at the very end of the bow straightening out.

Of course, many other more complex manoeuvres have been developed to deal with varying circumstances.

Early on in the season, the trout are down deep and not in any mood to chase their food. The only way to present a fly correctly here is at anchor. Either basic black or white work best now, with lures like Black Lure and its derivatives or the brilliant white Baby Doll perfect.

Anchor up and fish a slow sink or sink-tip line. After the lure hits the bottom, begin a slow retrieve. Often, takes come on only the second or third pull back, but sometimes they will follow the lure up through the water for a later take. If the fish are, as I would expect, hard on the bottom, switch to a fast sink line to save time.

Another early season choice, if you aren't keen on lure fishing, is a team of nymphs fished deep in a sheltered bay. Look for a bay with a nice ripple on the surface of the water and anchor up in around 15 feet of water. Use a leaded nymph on the point, to help sink the team — and fish it in exactly the same way as I described for the lure, with a slow, steady retrieve.

As the weather warms up a little, and fish begin to move, it is worth trying a slow inshore drift with either drogue or lee-board.

A sinktip is perfect for this, with a Black Chenille on the point and a nymph on the dropper. It's a combination of the two earlier methods, really, to allow you to check which tactic will work best on the more active fish. Don't start the retrieve until the fly has hit bottom, and keep the retrieve slow and steady.

Some of the best boat fishing can be had in June and July, as the warmer weather sends the fish on a daphnia feeding spree. Although the fish are always crammed to the gills with the tiny water fleas, they always seem ready to snap at anything that moves near to them. Maybe it's just aggression, brought on by the heavy feeding.

In these conditions, I like to cast across the breeze during a slow drogue-controlled drift. The lures want to be attractors, like Missionary, Appetizer or Jack Frost.

You will find little hotspots where the wind and current congregate the daphnia and the fish hang around. Drift until you find a hotspot and then really cash in on it.

Around the same time, you may notice little "bumps" on the surface of the water, where trout are taking nymphs just before they emerge from the water.

Now is the time to anchor up and change to a floating line in under 12 feet of water, or a sinktip in a deeper section of the reservoir. Whichever you use, you want the flies to fish deep, scraping the bottom. If, as is very likely, the trout are feeding on hatching sedges, there are many flies for the job.

They include the Sedge itself, Invicta, Amber Nymph, Wickham's Fancy, Ginger Quill, March Brown, Cinnamon and Gold and many more.

Use a long leader and grease it to within a few inches of the point fly — and don't grease the droppers. Start with flies tied on size 12 hooks, but be prepared to scale up to a ten or more if you prick and lose fish.

A good team would be an Invicta, Stick Fly or similar on the point, a Green and Brown Nymph on the first dropper, and an Amber Nymph on the top dropper.

I like to "skitter" the flies about just under the

Bob Church, the Northampton trout angler who has turned boat fishing for rainbows into a science. Big catches are the end result of skill, not chance.

surface on a short line — traditional loch style, if you like. Watch out, though. Fish hit hard with this method.

If the fish start taking those hatching flies with a splash, they are waiting until they are actually on the surface. Now is the time to fish right on the top. I like a dry Sedge on the point, but still keep the two nymphs skittering just under the surface.

An important point here is to remember not to strike too fast. The splash is often just the fish "drowning" the insect. He will come back again for the actual take, so wait until you see or feel the line tightening before you strike.

As summer draws on towards autumn, we see the start of the fry feeding, where the gaudiest of lures — patterns that would have scared fish silly earlier on — start producing big bags.

The fish seem to throw caution to the wind as the daphnia spree steps up. The sober black and white-based lures now give way to hot orange — with the Whisky Fly, Church Fry, Orange Muddler, Dunkeld and even Orange Baby Doll working well.

All the fish are in the top six feet of water, so tackle up with a sink tip or slow sink line and use a fast retrieve, without letting the lure sink too deep.

When fry feeding really starts to occupy fish, lures get bigger — four to five inches in length being nothing uncommon on some of the bigger reservoirs. Appetizers, Jack Frost, Muddler Minnow, Baby Doll, they all work well.

You want a fast sink line, especially a shooting head for longer casting and better action, a five yard leader, and those giant sized lures.

Wait until the line hits the bottom and watch out for very hard takes "on the drop". If they don't come, wait a moment and then give a long steady pull. If no take again, repeat the pull, just a little faster.

You are trying to induce a take by appealing to the aggression of the trout at this time. Annoy them, make them want to snap at this troublesome lure, and you are on your way to a limit of big fish.

Draycote

The biggest success story of any British trout reservoir in 1979 must belong to Warwickshire's Draycote Water.

After several years in the doldrums, with fish mysteriously failing to show up, anglers simply stopped fishing at the reservoir.

Then came the 1979 season, and Cinderella Draycote finally had the chance to show her true colours. The season started with a bang and just didn't let up. Journalists fishing the water's pre-season Press Day reported catching two and even three fish at a time on teams of flies.

The news soon travelled on the reservoir anglers' seemingly infallible "grapevine" and Draycote was packed on opening day.

The fish were still there, and they continued to be. Critics of the water had to learn to eat their words and all the "deserters" came guiltily back, like schoolboys after a days truancy.

For the rest of the season, Draycote continued to

Reservoir Figures:

Total catch 1978	Total to June 1979	Best brown 1978	Best brown 1979	Best rainbow 1978	Best rainbow 1979
13,299	15,990	6lb 2½oz	5lb 14oz	4lb 6½oz	4lb 9oz

show trout men that her former reputation as one of Britain's finest reservoir fisheries was well justified.

At the end of the 1978 season, many of the water's 32 fishing boats lay idle. To see ten out in a single day was a rare sight. But throughout 1979, open bookings have been harder to find than spots on the tail of a brown trout.

Many reservoirs suffered harshly at the hands of Britain's unsettled, and often freezing cold,

The scene at Draycote Water, a reservoir which has made an amazing comeback during the past twelve months. After a disastrous season, during which sport slumped for no apparent reason, catches have soared to record levels.

Spring. But not Draycote.

Even on the coldest days, visitors still managed to find their trout. And when May brought the first sun of the year, the trout went on a berserk feeding spree that just didn't end.

Those early men took their fish, mainly rainbows, on sinking lines and lures fished slowly across the bottom. But as May progressed, those Black Lures, Baby Dolls and Whisky Flies went back into the box. Out came floating lines, buzzers, nymphs and the more traditional wet fly patterns like Invicta, Mallard and Claret and Olive Dun. Some even caught on dry fly, as Draycote's famous fly hatches started to cloud the skies around the bank.

Most of the natural bank fished well, but for the real regulars, it was Toft Bay every time.

The early season rainbows were beautiful fish — bright, solid flashes of silver. The man in charge of fishing on the reservoir, Commander Robert Dunn, doesn't like black, ill-mended cock fish — so they all go back to the stews to mend for later stockings during the season.

By May, the brownies were active in the water, with four five-pounders topping the catches. The presence of those fish certainly knocked on the head the rumours that fish were dying off in Draycote as quickly as they were stocked.

Those big brownies had to be in the water during the problem years, along with hosts of their smaller cousins — so why had Draycote gone downhill so badly?

No-one knows the answer, though Commander Dunn and the Severn-Trent Water Authority are determined to find out the real reason for the decline. They have entered into a three or four year tagging programme to enable checks on growth rate, the food chain in the water, and hopefully even population estimates.

One change for 1979 was in the stocking policy. Draycote used to receive the bulk of its fish in the winter. Last season, Commander Dunn tried a new system, stocking a bulk 15,000 fish in the Spring, backed up by regular injections through the season.

It is too early to tell if this was at all relevant to the improved results of 1979, but the tagging programme and the next few years should help sort out the mystery.

Whatever the answer, the anglers had stopped worrying. They were cashing in on the best Draycote sport for years. By the middle of the season, they had already passed last year's total catch, and were returning an average of 2.2 fish per rod day — pretty good by any standard.

Grafham

The last few months of the 1978 trout season at Cambridgeshire's famed Grafham Water produced both extremes of Britain's fastest-growing branch of angling.

For an amazing eight week period saw reservoir fly fishing at its worst, with blanks as common as the fly hatches around the fishery, and then at its very best, with trout showing those almost suicidal tendencies normally reserved for the opening weeks of the season.

But before that glorious climax to what had started out as a great season, there was that barren six or seven week period; a period that had sent many anglers home scratching their heads — and fishless!

The fish were there, alright, as many as ever. But they just weren't feeding. Hundreds of anglers went through a few weeks of the frustrating experience and then packed up their tackle for the year.

They never knew why the fishing had died off. They simply cleaned up all their tackle and then packed it away until the next spring.

The anglers who stayed, including many die-hard regulars, discovered why the sport had died off. The reason was simple — snails.

Grafham Water was playing host to a massive snail migration. Millions of the tiny water creatures were moving across the giant reservoir, turning it into one of Britain's biggest trout "supermarkets".

The trout must have thought they had moved to a fish heaven. There was more natural food about than they had seen since those halcyon early seasons at Grafham, and they weren't about to let a chance like that slip by.

They cashed in on the bumper harvest, growing fat — and ignoring the seemingly endless list of fly patterns thrown at them by the frustrated anglers.

But then, with just a week of the season to go, the reservoir took off again. Boat men found the fish first. They were on top and feeding in a frenzy on what flies were still showing up in the rapidly cooling weather.

They were suckers for traditional tactics, short-lining on a long drift. Old favourites like Invicta, Wickhams, Cinnamon and Gold and other sedge patterns all took their share of fish.

The other main tactic that killed a lot of fish was more modern — casting a long line to the side of the boat and picking up the trout as the curve straightened out.

Most of the fish taken off the top with both methods were rainbows — and some of them beauties. But in Savage's Creek, it was a different story.

Boat anglers there started to pick up brown trout, with many of those brownies in the 4-5lb size range. Within a few days of the boat sport picking up, bank men found the trout, too.

The dam wall and all the natural bays, especially Savages Creek, fished well. Those men who had given up early had missed out on some of the best sport the season had to offer.

But if that season had gone out like the proverbial lion, the 1979 sport came in like the lamb.

Every trout water in Britain had experienced a slow start, thanks mainly to the harsh winter and unsettled Spring weather.

But Grafham had opened a lot later than most and still hit the same problems — even at a time when those early openers were starting to pick up a little.

The hundreds of anglers who had queued for opening day sport, and many of them had travelled from all parts of the country to be there, were very disappointed men.

Many didn't even see a fish to cast to, let alone catch. But the dam wall is always a good bet at the start of this season, and that at least provided some fish — even if they were only small stockies.

Even those fish didn't come easy, with a harsh wind blowing straight into the dam. Casting was difficult, even with heavy sinking lines. That pattern was repeated all over the water, with the savage north-westerly severely limiting possible fishing areas.

After the dam wall, the North Bank was probably the most popular venue for bank men, with black, white and orange lures working best during the day.

In the evenings, floating lines with a long leader and leaded Pheasant tail on the point also produced odd fish. What fish were taken were black, ill-mended, rainbows.

Boat anglers, when they could safely get out, recorded poor returns with just a few fish from the depths of the trolling area and Gaynes Lode.

As May progressed, the slightly warmer weather produced better catches — but not by much. The south end of the dam and around the area of G buoy produced stockies through the day, while the bigger fish started to move from the Church Hill Farm bank to Savages Creek.

Bank and boat men stuck with basic white lure patterns in the day, switching to a floating line, buzzers and green and brown nymphs.

Boat sport picked up steadily, though the wind still made fishing difficult at times. Valley Creek and Perry Point joined the slowly growing list of fish producers, especially in the evening.

Buzzers still worked well on a floating line, with many anglers adding a Stick Fly to the point. Lure men, meanwhile, were finding fish in the trolling areas on larger Black Lures.

Stockie rainbows moved over the north end of the dam across to the tower, with those favourite Black Lures still finding some browns and rainbows in the 3-4lb class. Bank men, willing to walk the distance to Savages Creek, had good evening sport with buzzers.

By the end of the month, boat anglers were starting to catch fish on the top, using slow-sink or floating lines and traditional patterns like Wickham's Fancy and Dunkeld.

With the much warmer weather of June, trout had spread over most of Grafham, though catches were still limited. And then came the daphnia blooms, which soon pre-occupied the trout.

They almost disappeared again. Even the evening rises failed to materialise and sport slowed right down again.

One interesting thing did happen in June, though. During a routine netting operation to remove pike, bailiffs turned up a 33 inch brown trout. That brownie, estimated at 14lb, was returned to the water.

That sort of occurrence shows the quality that Grafham is capable of — but that didn't really help anglers in the 1979 season.

Northamptonshire angler Jon Jessop with a superb 9lb 4oz brownie taken from Valley Creek.

Reservoir Figures:

Total catch 1978	Total to June 1979	Best brown 1978	Best brown 1979	Best rainbow 1978	Best rainbow 1979
36,710	8,153	9lb 6½oz	7lb 15oz	6lb 4oz	5lb

Ron Burgin

Midland Stillwater Ace

Like coarse angling master Ivan Marks, Ron Burgin, a Nottingham engineer, has an amazing capacity for remembering statistics. Who caught what, where, how and on what are vital snippets of information to Ron, who at 28, is rapidly becoming established as a trout angler to watch.

"Most forget these little bits of news almost as soon as they hear them, or fail to question further an angler who has enjoyed a successful day. Remembering all this information prevents a great deal of wasted effort. For instance if one or two very good anglers tell you that they failed to catch because the wind changed, or it was colder than usual on a particular piece of water, then obviously that area is to be avoided when the same circumstances occur again. The same goes for all the different lures and flies."

Everything that Ron hears all goes down in a diary. It is filled with information gathered over six seasons. A glance through before his next trip puts him in the best area and with the most killing lure at the end of his leader.

He remembers his first trout fishing trip vividly. "It was to Eye Brook. The buzzers were hatching in clouds and although I had plenty of pulls caught nothing then or for the next six visits. Even so I discovered that trout fishing was for me. It had something I had never found in coarse angling."

Unlike most newcomers to stillwater trouting' Ron began with a light rod, a floating line and a box of nymphs.

"I teamed up with Steve Parton who had advertised for a companion to share the travelling costs. We went along to hear Arthur Cove give one of his famous Grafham lectures. We were fascinated. That season we averaged 3.5 trout a visit on nymph fishing tactics."

The partnership broke up briefly and Ron, in his thirst for other styles, switched his attentions to deep fishing for Grafham's big brown trout. He was one of the first to use the lead-cored line, a tactic which has more than its share of critics but also an equally large number of converts.

He developed a way of swinging the lead line across the bottom which was anything but a hurling out and a pulling back of a garish lure.

His deep swing style has brought Ron several brown trout over 5lb. His best brown so far from Rutland weights 5lb 4oz.

His success rate can perhaps be better judged in terms of blank outings. He has suffered but two in the last five seasons.

Most of Ron's fishing is based from a boat. He prefers the solitude it brings and the ability to change the scenery with a touch of the starter button.

He regards the boat angler's most important asset as his partner. Find an angler you can really get on with and who shares your own fishing views and then stick to him is Ron's advice. His own regular boat partner is the angler he began with — Steve Parton from Nottingham. Ron's views on stillwater anglers are certain to raise a few hackles.

"Most are idle and almost expect the fish to jump on the bank because they have paid the price of a day ticket. All they have done is pay for the right to fish. The rest is up to them."

One of the biggest mistakes made by many anglers is not to analyse their own fishing. "Far too many sit back and then blame Lady Luck when the answer to their problems is, on most occasions, right in front of their eyes. It is all a question of asking the right questions of those who do know and then remembering what they said.

The two men I regard as the very best stillwater anglers are Dick Shrive and Arthur Cove. Both their attitudes and styles are totally different and yet both share the same ability to look, learn and then improve."

Ron reacts fiercely to the accusation that he is a one method angler. "To me fishing is all about catching fish. If the fish want it deep then that is where I fish."

"If they want it on the surface or in mid water then that is where I focus my attention. I fish all styles and of all methods I still prefer to take fish on light gear and nymphs. At the same time I like to see fish in the net. After all what's the point of fishing a tiny fly on the surface when the trout are 30 feet below eating fry a couple of inches long?"

His work rate, like that of Bob Church, is phenomenal. Every trout provides a challenge. And, for those who like counting, Ron has recorded seven trout a trip over the past five seasons.

Ron Burgin displays a fine brace of trout taken from a hard-fished Midlands reservoir. By carefully gathering information Ron has built up a reputation as one of the most successful trout anglers in the country.

Big Brownies by Dave Allen

I don't think there is anything in modern stillwater trouting with more magic and mystery than hunting for big brown trout. The thrill of those savage takes transmitted up the line to the rod, and those long, powerful runs, has to be felt to be believed.

I have caught my share of decent brownies, but I still marvel at every one. But first of all, let's get things in perspective. While those big browns are by no means impossible to catch, they are no pushover either.

There are a lot of ways, though, to increase your chances of contacting these exciting fish. And one of the most important is location. Every water has its own hotspots, usually in the deeper areas, and it can take a while to build up a sound knowledge of the top marks.

But if the water is new to you, a few pints bought for a regular can save a lot of time and trouble.

Then comes caution and skill. Brown trout, unlike their short-lived cousin, the rainbow, can live for 15 or 20 years or more. If they have survived that long, you can bet they have seen every trick in the book over the years. They are wary and have an uncanny skill in avoiding capture.

There are times, of course, when they seem to throw caution to the wind and act more like suicidal stockies, but these are few and far between.

First of all, boat men have a much better chance of contacting the fish. Unlike rainbows, they feed mostly at night, returning to the depths for the daylight hours.

I have often caught browns with leeches clinging to their sides, showing how hard they hug the bottom during the day. But as very few waters allow night fishing, especially on the major reservoirs, we are usually restricted to specialised boat tactics — and patience really is a virtue.

The main reason for success at this time is that the brownie is a very aggressive and territorial creature. You can't tempt him because he is hungry, but you can goad him into attacking anything that invades his territory — including your lure.

Let's take a typical season and look at good areas and tactics for the different stages. Early on, you will often find the browns still hanging around the feeder streams after spawning.

They are ravenous after the winter's activities and roving the freshly flooded margins for easy pickings among the drowned worms and insects. This is one time when the bank men can cash in.

One of the trout's favourite meals at this time is the creamy-white grub of the Daddy-Long-Legs. So obviously, a Baby Doll is the perfect pattern early on. Fish a slow sink line and a lure tied on a size eight or ten long shank. The Black Lure is also useful now, as it imitates the slugs that have been

A double-figure trout, taken from Grafham, on a lead core line

washed into the water.

Inch the lure very slowly across the bottom — a figure of eight retrieve is just the right rate. Takes can vary a lot. Often, they are the gentlest of plucks as the trout is used to picking up half-drowned insects and isn't expecting any trouble. But sometimes they hit the lure like a rocket — so be prepared.

Don't point the rod straight down the line. You will be broken hopelessly on every smash take. Instead, fish "sideways on" so the rod can take the sting out of the take.

As the weather starts to warm up, and after the trout have eaten enough to recover their strength, they start to move out into their deepwater lies. They still return to the shallows at night to feed, and with a good buzzer hatch the bank man still has the chance of good sport.

The trouble here is that there are usually twice as many rainbows competing for your fly. You just can't guarantee big brownies.

Now is the time Aquasink and lead core lines start to come into their own. When you have located the area you think holds some brownies, drift the boat over it with a drogue or, preferably, a lee-board or tiller.

Cast out and let your lure sink to the bottom. The fish are a lot livelier by now, so you can speed up the retrieve to what I would call average — long steady pulls, taking in a foot or so of line each time.

If the fish don't hit the lure as it passes their nose, they will often follow it up through the water, sometimes "tapping" it repeatedly. When this happens, there are several things you can do. First of all, speed up the retrieve. Make the fish angry and induce it to strike.

If you still get plucks but can't make contact, scale down the size of the lure — after making sure the hook point is razor sharp.

The size of lure is something for you to decide, depending on the conditions, but I think the bigger the better. Size six long shanks are not uncommon, even tied tandem — and tube flies are catching on in a big way. I like something along the lines of a Black Chenille for this style of fishing. Any basic dark lures with a bit of flash will work as well.

During May and June, the towers on any reservoir are big fry holding spots — and the trout are never far away. Both browns and rainbows are crashing through the fry shoals, but there is a way to try and avoid rainbows.

Usually, they attack the shoals high in the water, so a fast stripped lure near the top will attract them. The browns prefer to hang much lower in the water, often living off the rainbows "leftovers" — dead and dying fish dropping down through the water.

Here, long shank eights and sixes are needed, and the lure needs a bit of feather to make it flutter down through the water like a dying fish. Appetizers, Missionary, Jack Frost and Muddler all have their place here. Use a slow sink line, even in the deepest waters.

Takes often come on the drop. You can't miss them as the line starts peeling off your reel and the fish turns away with his catch. Don't be in a hurry to strike; like pike they often turn the lure, so wait a few seconds to be sure of contact.

If you haven't had a take on the drop, just "twitch" the line in a slow retrieve to imitate a dying fry struggling to get back to the surface. If that doesn't work, either, use a lead core line and strip the lure back across the bottom as fast as you can. The takes are unbelievably violent, so be prepared for fireworks.

For this type of fishing, old hands often use stepped-up carp rod blanks — so don't expect to land much on your nymphing gear here. Leaders need to be at least 7lb, and are often scaled up to 9lb or more.

About this time, the browns also start moving back inshore for the heavy rises of first buzzers and then sedges. Sedge time in July and August produces some of the best sport of the season and also gives the bank man another chance to hit big fish.

Fish a floating line, greased leader and any big sedge pattern — Invicta, the common Sedge, Pheasant Tail, Cinnamon and Gold, etc. Or if the fish are feeding on the nymphs just below the surface, fish a Sedge Pupa on an ungreased leader. Either way, fish with quick six inch pulls and be prepared for smash takes.

The back end of the season is always the best time for brownie fishing, for they seem to throw caution to the wind as they eat anything they can find to pack on weight ready for the coming winter.

They are after the big fry and feed throughout the day. I have seen brownies throw themselves onto a dam wall in their frenzy to smash up the fry shoals.

Sport will be intermittent. After a few minutes' frenzied feeding, the trout will go back to deeper water to digest their meal before coming in for another foray — so when you find them, sit out the lean spells.

The feeding sprees will more than make up for the breaks. Fish patterns like Polystickle, Appetizer, Baby Doll or Muddler, and fish exactly as I described for fry feeders around the towers earlier in the year.

Packington

Packington, set in the heart of the Warwickshire countryside, is one of those trout fisheries where anglers have come to expect a new record catch almost every year. And she hasn't failed to oblige her supporters yet — though the last few years have made the fishery work hard to live up to its amazing reputation.

The 1976 drought had its effect, an effect that was felt the following year, too. In 1978 a new problem arose. With the fishery one of the earliest to open in Britain — on March 18 — regulars at Packington are used to a cold start to their fishing.

But the early Spring of 1978 was something else. Boats had to be chipped free of the ice-bound margins and anglers, loaded with several sets of extra clothing, had problems with lines icing up in their rod rings. Sales of soup rocketed at the fishery and thermal underwear became all the vogue.

Although relatively slow, catches on all of Packington's famous trout pools were steadily consistent. By the halfway stage of the season, catches were marginally better than the trouble-torn previous year — though in those freezing conditions that was incredible in itself.

After the initial rush during the opening weeks, attendance dropped off while all but the keenest anglers adjourned their sport until the arrival of better weather. But that was a long time coming.

When the sun finally made an appearance, anglers returned in their hundreds and the catch rate soared. It went up so well, in fact, that Packington was able to set another new catch record — with 23,548 fish, more than 5,000 above the 1977 figures.

The fishery's extra long season, until November 15 — and its ability to produce fish right up until closing day — played a big part in those remarkable new figures.

Fishery manager, Lord Guernsey, attributed much of the success, in the most difficult of conditions, to the new stocking policy brought in at Packington that year. Out went the large scale injections of fish at regular intervals, and in came little-and-often stockings on a classic put and take style.

As well as ensuring regular topping up with fresh fish, the method helped give an extra measure of control over all aspects of fishery management.

Throughout the ravages of winter, fishery managers all over Britain were more than a little nervous about the prospects for the 1979 opening — and with a March 18 deadline, Lord Guernsey must have had a few more worries than most.

But he needn't have worried. Anglers did fish in snowstorms, but that was nothing new in the Forest of Arden. The important thing was that they did bother to turn out. And, even more important, so did the fish.

Despite the appalling conditions in March, fish were feeding — albeit slowly. Sport was patchy, but strong enough to hold visitors' attention and make them want to go back for more.

Sinking lines and lures, especially the basic colour variations of black and white, produced fish more steadily than anyone had hoped for in the cold weather. Sport stayed slow right through the first eight weeks of the season, but by mid-May

A peaceful evening scene on one of Packington's small, shallow pools. During the last few seasons Packington has established a reputation for consistency with new record catch totals being set up year after year, on the no-limit water.

things started to liven up a little.

Packington Fishery, of course, consists of a series of small, shallow, pools — no more than 12 to 14 feet of water at their deepest points, and considerably less over most of the acreage.

So it doesn't take as much sun as it would on the much bigger public reservoirs to warm up the water and liven up sport. Daytime sport was still patchy, but the hot sun that turned up on odd days warmed the water sufficiently by the evening to see fly hatches.

Sparse at first, they increased slowly as the weather warmed. Those hatches, together with a

steady supply of new stock fish, really set things moving on all the pools. Fish were still hard to tempt, but some regulars had a reasonable amount of success with a small Black Buzzer stripped across the surface on a floating line at dusk.

Daytime visitors stuck to black and white lures, especially the Black and Peacock Spider that has grown so well loved at Packington. A new innovation, the lime green Baby Doll, also appeared regularly in the visitors' book among the Black Lures and Sweeney Todds.

Another useful tactic was to fish a floating line with a long leader, allowing the wind to work a single Pheasant Tail Nymph or Black Buzzer. Towards the end of May it was much warmer, though still a bit unpredictable, and sport improved even more. All pools produced fish, with trout to 3lb rising well.

Those evening rises improved steadily but the fish were still no pushovers, and the single stripped buzzer still worked best.

The trout started to respond a little better to colour in the daytime and some regulars had reasonable success with a variety of black and yellow-based lures. Some big bags were taken including one great haul of 22 fish from Broadwater at the end of May.

As May moved into June, small hatches of olives started to occur and the fish moved right into the margins for this new food supply. Careful casting with a team of Olive Nymphs now started to pay off. A long leader and slow, inching retrieve, was needed.

The fish continued to rise, but the increased bank pressure soon moved the trout out from the margins. The most successful method was then long casting with a lime green Baby Doll on a floating line.

Big fish were still noticeable by their absence. The best rainbow by mid-season was a 3lb 10oz fish from Great Pool, and the top brownie went just 2¾lb. That fish came from Hall Stew, one of the old holding pools opened up for members-only fishing in 1979.

The best bag in the first half of the season was one of 34 fish taken off Broadwater, though a number of other anglers pushed that record hard.

Reservoir Figures:

Total catch 1978	Total by June 1979	Best brown 1978	Best brown 1979	Best rainbow 1978	Best rainbow 1979
23,548	12,499	4lb 10oz	2lb 12oz	4lb 10oz	3lb 10oz

Eye Brook

The unsettled weather at the start of the 1979 season hit Northamptonshire's Eye Brook Reservoir a little harder than most, with thick, muddy water making fishing very difficult.

The poor start was a real anti-climax, especially for those anglers who had seen out the previous season on the reservoir. As usual, Eye Brook had rallied for a magnificent tail-end bonanza, with almost 10,000 trout from half that number of rods in the last two months of fishing.

And that tremendous run of fish produced new record fish per rod day figures of 1.46. Since the opening of giant neighbour Rutland Water, Eye Brook seems to have settled with a regular 15,000 to 16,000 visits a year.

Unlike other trout reservoirs in the area, Eye Brook doesn't seem to have suffered a big walk out from regulars keen to transfer their loyalties to the new boy.

It is possibly a measure of the interest that so many trout men still have in the more traditional style fishing offered by Eye Brook.

There were no giants landed in 1978, but regulars enjoyed consistent sport with the 23,096 trout landed. And those figures include 1,314 fish over 2lb, topped by a 4lb rainbow and 4¾lb brown trout.

For the statistically-minded, those 23,096 trout made up 94 per cent of the total number of fish stocked into the reservoir during the year.

And it is interesting to see that Eye Brook has, over the past five years, managed to maintain a consistently high fish caught to fish stocked ratio.

1974 : 94 per cent.
1975 : 89 per cent.
1976 : 89 per cent.
1977 :102 per cent.
1978 : 98 per cent.

Obviously, that 102 per cent figure in 1977 included fish stocked in previous years. But after that magnificent closing in 1978, anglers who lined the banks of Eye Brook on the following year's opening day were due for a disappointing start to their season's fishing.

With the late opening — March 30 instead of the usual March 23 start — anglers had already lost a week's fishing and were obviously keen to get started.

But their happy memories of the previous season soon disappeared in the brown murk that was Eye Brook.

Regulars on the reservoir have an age-old enemy — the North East Wind. The valley that houses the picturesque 400 acre fishery acts like a purpose-built wind tunnel for those north-easterlies. And many anglers have given up under the strain of trying to fish against it.

A beaten trout slides towards the waiting net.

But in 1979, the wind was at its worst for many years — and it had allies. The long, cold winter had left its mark. Freezing water temperatures weren't encouraging trout to feed. And any that did had a lot of trouble finding an angler's lure in water that was more like Windsor Soup.

And as if that wasn't enough, the early weeks also suffered under almost a month of torrential rain.

Trout were very few and far between in those early days. Even regulars who could fairly be described as Eye Brook experts went home empty-handed.

Many eventually transferred their long-suffering allegiance to other waters in the area. But then the weather started improving. The

After a slow start sport rapidly improved.

winds died down, the water temperature slowly climbed up the thermometer, and the water cleared.

It wasn't an overnight change, but it wasn't long before catches started to improve. The old faithfuls were rewarded for their efforts as the trout began to feed.

The fishery management, encouraged by the obvious improvement, helped Nature along with extra stocking of bright new rainbow trout — guaranteed to start the old fish moving.

The people who had stuck it out — if only because they had regular boat bookings paid for and didn't want to throw their money away completely — started catching the trout that had frustrated them so much earlier in the season.

They had stuck to their guns, scratching the odd trout out on a small black lure. Often they had gone home empty-handed, but their belief in the water made many of them return.

Then, in mid-May, things started to improve for them. The bank anglers, especially, started catching trout — and plenty of them.

Half a dozen fish per angler was common and anything up to a dozen glistening trout wasn't a rare sight. Most of those early fish were the stockie rainbows, but plenty of brown trout were turning up too. Their decision to feed was heralded in the middle of May, and highlighted by the capture of a 3lb 3oz brownie on May 19.

Eye Brook was now back on its feet and fighting hard to regain lost ground. Six weeks of the season had been virtually lost and there was a lot of making-up to do.

And the fishery managed it. Despite all the problems, by mid-June Eye Brook had practically equalled the catch figures for the same period in the previous year.

Boat sport had picked up considerably, and bank anglers were enjoying a real trout bonanza.

Catches soared, and Leicester visitor Ron Bower set a new season's best with 23 rainbows from one boat trip. And as if that wasn't enough, he went back a week later and set a new target for the season's best rainbow trout with a 5lb fish.

And to prove it was no fluke, the reservoir quickly followed up with another five-pounder, this time by Corby local Alan Wallis.

Those lures had been returned to the fly boxes as fish moved constantly on the surface of the water. And the fish were on the move all the time. No sooner had the Rutland Bank gained the reputation as the best spot, that the Leicester Bank or Dam Wall started to produce as many fish.

As always, Eye Brook plodded on through all her difficulties, producing a steady run of fish. That is why she manages to hold so many regulars spellbound every year.

Reservoir Figures:

Total catch 1978	Total to June 1979	Best brown 1978	Best brown 1979	Best rainbow 1978	Best rainbow 1979
23,096	6,428	4lb 12oz	4lb 4oz	4lb	5lb

Welsh Waters

Mention Wales to a cross-section of trout anglers and then stand back and study. Watch for that far-away look through misty eyes as they think of the home of British game fishing.

And anyone who still believes that Eye Brook is the ultimate in traditional fishing on these islands should visit the Principality.

Tame, stew-fed, rainbows are still virtually unheard of — though they are creeping slowly into a growing number of put and take fisheries. No, it is the pure, sparkling and fighting-fit wild brownie that most Welshmen pit their wits against.

Sport with those butter-bellied beauties can be hard, but the Welsh grow up to accept that as a simple fact of life.

And, despite the fact that they spurn the many modern methods that have sprung up in recent years on the richer new waters over the border in England, their own traditional armoury of tactics serves them well.

That holds true in even the leanest of times, when those stockie rainbows sulk in their black spawning mantle, refusing to feed.

Although 1978 proved to be a real problem year for most Welsh waters, it was an eventful year, too. It saw the opening of the hilly country's biggest ever stillwater fishery, the thousand acre Llyn Brenig, in North Wales.

Brenig opened with a storm of catches and then, just as quickly, sport died off. Many mystified and disappointed anglers turned to other waters. But then things improved and by mid-summer the anglers were back.

From there, Brenig grew from strength to strength to finish up as a real showpiece for the Welsh Water Authority.

Then, down in South Wales, Glamorgan's Llwyn-on Reservoir set a new Welsh record with a 13lb 1oz rainbow. News of the amazing catch from a previously little-known water reached far across the border and fired the imaginations of even the hardened big-fish men from Northamptonshire.

They invaded Glamorgan with a full armoury, including drogues, lee-boards, lead core lines and giant-sized lures. Welshmen looked on in horror as the invaders attacked their new hotspot. But the horror turned to fascination as they realised how well these strange new tactics worked.

It also opened the eyes of the visiting English, who at last began to realise that Wales, although still a traditionalist's stronghold, was keeping pace with the modern world — in its own way.

That 13-pounder was a big brood fish stocked specially to add spice to the water. But the lead core lines attracted a lot more fish in the five to 6lb class and even bigger — fish the Welsh had begun to think of as legends, turning up only often enough to keep the stories going.

But apart from the odd highlights, there was little to distinguish Welsh sport in 1978. Even the late openers started slowly and stayed that way — with only restocking giving short periods of grace from the steady doldrums.

One water that did shine, though, was the Central Electricity Board's Ffestiniog Fishery in North Wales.

Despite losing its jealously-guarded Welsh rainbow record to Llwyn-on, the water managed to top its own former best five times in that single season.

The best was a 12-pounder landed in August by Knutsford, Cheshire, angler Ken Fox. At the present time, Ffestiniog boasts six of the top seven rainbows ever recorded from Wales.

The 1979 season started slowly, throughout the whole of Wales. With the traditionally earlier

A picturesque scene at Brenig, the Welsh Water Authority's new showpiece reservoir. The 1,000 acre water now provides first-class sport.

opening dates than the rest of Britain, the savage winter made its mark more quickly and more obviously.

One of the first off the mark was Ffestiniog. So successful during the previous season, it suffered badly during those early, snow-filled weeks.

Opening day provided a few high spots, though, including an 8½lb rainbow. Like most early trout, it fell for legered worm. In fact, the use of bait like worms and maggots is almost certainly what set Ffestiniog above its fly-only neighbours.

By June, the fishery had produced a total of four fish over 8lb, but only one fell to a fly fisherman. The others fell, one each, to worm, spinner and maggot.

The catches also included 15 fish over 7lb and several hundred in the 5-6lb class. Water temperature is very critical to fly fishermen at Ffestiniog and it wasn't until early May that the water hit the vital level of 7 degrees Centigrade.

Elsewhere, the picture was exactly the same, with poor early season catches. Anglers who braved the snow and late frosts did find some trout by easing small black lures across the bottom, but no-one was catching consistently anywhere.

But Welsh fly fishermen are a patient breed and they stuck at it. In the Welsh Water Authority put and take fisheries, especially in the highly populated South Wales area, regular injections of ignorant new stockie rainbows kept things ticking over — but only just, and with short-lived success.

The unpredictable weather prevented any set pattern of feeding, for the tacticians to work on, but by mid-May, heavy downpours of rain had coloured most waters — and flashy attractors started to work.

Anglers cashed in on the long-awaited sport with sinking lines and fly patterns like Butcher, Alexandra and Peter Ross.

Then, as May progressed, bank anglers started to find fish in the margins, feeding cautiously on the sparse buzzer hatches late in the evening.

Teams of buzzers and nymphs worked reasonably well in the warmer breaks in the weather, but the frequent cold snaps saw sport restricted to boat men fishing deep with Baby Doll, Black Lure, White Maribou and sometimes the Whisky Fly.

Only the now frequent injections of new stock made any water really start to move, and that was about the only pattern able to establish itself in Wales during the 1979 season.

Nymphing by Frank Cutler

In these days of high pressure reservoir fishing, two inch lures are commonplace — and some patterns as long as four or even five inches are by no means a rare sight.

Now I don't like fishing with that sort of thing. I don't knock the people who do, though, as in fishing it's very much a case of each to his own. I just prefer a more pleasant and satisfying way of catching my trout — and that is nymphing.

With many of today's new reservoir men being brought up on a diet of Black Lures, Baby Dolls and Appetizers, the old arts are in danger of dying out. Though I am certain that today's lure men will be tomorrow's nymph fishermen if only because they discover it is a far more pleasant way of taking trout.

If I hear that tired old argument, that only lures catch the big fish, one more time I will start to give up on the future of trout fishing. Of course lures catch big fish, but so do nymphs. Hardly a year goes by at Grafham, for instance, without at least one near double figure fish falling to a nymph. And I haven't heard any Rutland nymph regulars complaining, either.

The thing is that this method needs a little more skill and care than any other. But as people tire of dragging lures through the water, it is the natural progression to make.

First of all, let us talk about the sort of tackle you need. The rod is obviously crucial. The average 9ft reservoir rod can be used, though I prefer something a little longer, say ten feet.

This extra length is very important for a number of reasons. First of all, it enables you to keep the line well up in the air. This avoids snagging the bank with every other back cast, especially with the slightly longer leaders used in nymphing. It also gives a valuable extra bit of lift at the end of each retrieve.

How often have you retrieved a team of nymphs only to have a trout snatch at a fly just as you are lifting the line from the water? And how often have you missed that last-second take?

What happens is that a trout will often follow a team of flies right in to the bank. His curiosity is aroused, but he is still cautious.

Then he sees his "prey" about to leave the water, just as a natural nymph does, and pounces. You are already clearing the line from the water quite quickly ready for the next cast, and you pull the hook from the trout's mouth.

Always fish a retrieve right out, gently lifting the team of nymphs clear of the water before putting on the power to re-cast. Many of the season's biggest brownies are taken this way on waters all over the country, especially when they take to cruising close in during the late summer and autumn.

That extra long rod gives you the chance to lift the team out in the right way and still be ready to cast to a fish you have spotted moving.

The reel is relatively unimportant, as its main function is simply as a line holder. But that line is probably your most important item of tackle. Don't skimp on this if you want the best results.

Your line is everything. It is what takes your nymphs out to the feeding fish, what holds them up in the water, and usually what signals your take as well.

Cheaper lines don't usually have the proper weight or balance for the best casting and presentation. So buy the best line you can afford — and don't be afraid to ask a local tackle dealer or your local expert for advice. And make sure it is rated for the rod you use.

You obviously want a floating line, and I find a double taper the best all-rounder. And you can always change it round every season to minimise wear on any one end.

If you can afford it, there are times when a forward taper line will help in casting, and sometimes even a floating shooting head can be used to advantage.

There are many different types and styles of leaders, or casts, on the market. Tapered leaders seem to have grown immensely in popularity, and they can sometimes help a lot.

But they can cause tangles for the beginner, and a good level nylon is perfect for the job anyway. I like a 6lb breaking strain for the big reservoirs, with length anything from ten feet to 15 feet or more, depending on the conditions.

The selection of nymphs and buzzers is too wide and varied to try and cover here, though I will specify good patterns and sizes for some of the methods I describe.

But first you must decide where to fish. I like to find a bank with the wind blowing from left to right along the bank. But I am right-handed and a "southpaw" might prefer it the other way around.

With the wind in this direction, the water refraction helps to hide me, and the wind itself keeps the line tight and moves the team of nymphs in as near a natural way as possible.

On a rough day, especially, you can let the wind do all the work for you. Don't bother to retrieve at all, let the wind work the flies.

When you have found a likely-looking spot, look at the water. If fish are showing on the top, fish right on the top. If none are showing, fish deeper down.

If the fish are down, I like a 12 foot leader, longer

A fine catch of reservoir trout taken on the nymph by Frank Cutler.

if the water is much deeper. Fish a team of three nymphs tied on size eight hooks. Space them evenly on three or four inch droppers. This gives an equal rate of sink for improved presentation.

Cast out as far as you comfortably can and let the ungreased leader sink completely.

Hold the rod tip two feet above the water and point it straight down the line. The retrieve should be slow, inching the team gently along the bottom — a figure of eight retrieve gives the perfect speed.

If it isn't too windy, watch the end of the fly line for a sign of a take. If it's too windy for that, watch the line between the rod tip and the water — it acts like the swingtip so familiar to coarse anglers.

Either way, you are looking for a forward movement of the line. It could be the slightest inching forward or a really bold pull. Either way, tighten up firmly by raising the rod tip. There is no need for an extravagant strike, which can sometimes pull the hook free — especially on those gentle plucking takes.

If the fish are rising, and this is signalled by a slight boil in the water — splashing rises are fish feeding on dry fly, so ignore them with a nymph — I prefer a shorter leader.

Use a ten foot leader with just two flies, this time size tens. Work out the direction a fish is heading into by following the path of the boils — usually into the wind — and drop the flies about a yard ahead of the last boil.

This calls for fairly accurate casting, especially in calm conditions, for the sight of the actual fly line in front of his nose will scare the stupidest trout.

Start a faster retrieve immediately you hit the water. Let the flies sink and you will be fishing below the feeding fish. The takes here are usually hard. On those real problem days, the flat oily calm, nymphing is about the only method that will work.

Go again for two nymphs, or even just one. The important thing now is to keep weight down, so one fly is best. The fish, which you see heading and tailing are in the top six inches of water — and that is where your flies must be to catch them.

Grease the leader to within a few inches of the fly. If you do use a dropper, don't grease that. And go down to a size 12 hook, again to help cut down weight. Cast to the fish and retrieve slowly and carefully — the slightest wake could ruin everything.

In these conditions, with the slightest ripple, put a dry fly on the top dropper and your nymph on the point. The dry fly acts like a float, holding up the nymph, and sometimes even signals the take for you.

West Country Waters

Those American brook trout that first set the West Country trout fishing world alight back in 1977 did it again the following year — and then again in 1979.

Within hours of the 1978 opening day at the South West Water Authority's Trenchford Reservoir, near Moreton Hampstead, in Devon, local man Tony Clarke had established a new British record for the species when a 3lb 2oz brookie fell for his deep-fished Whisky Fly.

Hampshire's famed Avington Fishery then jumped on the brookie bandwagon and dominated the record list with a series of fish finally topped by a 4lb 10oz trout.

Or they did until the 1979 season started in the south west. Again, within hours of the start, the brookie record had tumbled to a Devon angler.

This time, the water was Fernworthy, which was to take over from Trenchford as the South West Water Authority's brook trout centrepiece.

A scenic West Country water. The introduction of brook trout has proved remarkably successful.

This time round, the record went twice on opening day — first with a 4lb 15oz fish and then with Dolton, Devon, angler John Sunman's 5lb 5oz beauty. Those opening day catches at Fernworthy also included seven other fish between 3lb 6oz and 3lb 12oz . . . and the following day produced another 4lb plus brookie.

The water authority were well pleased with the results, because Fernworthy has long been a problem water for them. With an even higher pH level than their other acid waters, brown and rainbow trout have a job to survive in the reservoir.

But a delayed opening date, until May 28, and a massive brook trout stocking saw a "useless" water transformed into a leading specialist fishery.

The Authority also stepped up brook trout stocking at their other put and take waters — except Kennick — to supplement the rainbow stocks in the early part of the season.

When other fish are still sulking in the cold weather, brookies seem to respond well to all methods of fly fishing.

Trout men in Devon and Cornwall had a lot to live up to after the West Country's fabulous 1978 season — a year that included a new Authority rainbow record at 14lb 2oz. Even the special winter fisheries — Argal, Upper Tamar and Kennick — fished well. No giants were taken, but catch figures were substantially up on previous winters.

The special extension runs from October 12 right up to Christmas Eve on all three waters, but disappointing December results may see future snow sport curtailed at the end of November. Kennick, especially, saw many more winter visitors as the M5 made access easy from Bristol.

Generally speaking, 1979 started slowly at most Devon and Cornwall fisheries. The long, harsh winter and unsettled spring weather weren't helping things at all.

The brown trout, usually the first to queue for food, hardly showed up at all. Rainbows were thin on the ground, though the brook trout supplemented them well.

The unsettled weather continued until mid-May — holding the fishing down with it. Then, slowly at first, things started to liven up a bit. The brook trout were slowing down as their numbers were thinned out, but rainbows started to move on all waters.

Catches soon improved from less than one fish per rod day to two or even more at some waters.

Porth, especially, had been slow to respond to the sun, but by the end of May, the fish per rod average had trebled.

Throughout the 1979 season, though, the big fish, for which the south west has become famous, were noticeably absent. Water Authority staff blamed the poor recovery rate after spawning on the terrible weather conditions. The big fish simply were not on hand for stocking.

Most waters managed to top the 6lb mark before long, though, with Kennick taking the lead in mid-June with an 8lb rainbow.

Anglers who had lined snow-lined banks, scraping lures across the bottom for the odd fish, moved first to buzzers and nymphs and quickly to the Hawthorne Fly imitations that work so well in this area in the summer. The hatches of those, and the sedges, were magnificent at most waters.

The prospects for next year look even brighter, especially with the new Wimbleball Reservoir due to open on May 1. The 374 acre fishery, near Dulverton, on Exmoor, should provide some fabulous sport. The first trout were introduced in early 1978, so two years' growth in a rich new water should see some heavyweights moving around.

Reservoir Figures:

	Total catch 1978	Total to June 1979	Best brown 1978	Best brown 1979	Best rainbow 1978	Best rainbow 1979
Argal	5,065	2,752	—	2lb 1oz	13lb 14oz	6lb 3oz
Porth	3,436	1,476	—	—	13lb 14oz	6lb 9oz
Siblyback	7,862	4,231	3lb 4oz	3lb 2oz	12lb 9oz	6lb 8oz
Upper Tamar	8,803	4,146	3lb 8oz	2lb 8oz	12lb 5oz	6lb 4oz
Wistlandpound	3,244	2,013	3lb 8oz	—	14lb 2oz	6lb 5oz
Fernworthy	3,359	1,561	—	—	6lb 14oz	—
Kennick	12,179	5,194	3lb	—	2lb 2oz	8lb

Southern Waters

Yet another trout is brought to the net at the Southern Water Authority's fabulous Bewl Bridge reservoir. In its first season, the reservoir produced nearly 100,000 trout.

When Bewl Bridge Reservoir opened in Kent for the first time in 1978, it revolutionised trout fishing in the south — and attracted a flood of complaints from anglers.

But the staff of this Southern Water Authority reservoir weren't at all alarmed, for the "complaints" were that fish were too easy to catch. And easy they were, with even the rawest beginner able to take a limit in a fairly short time.

Relatively useful fly fishermen could, at times, find their quota filled after literally only a few minutes' fishing. The fish were everywhere, and greedily grabbing anything cast at them by even the most inept novice.

Everything from a tiny nymph to lures, tied on hooks as large as size six long shank, were hit by the seemingly suicidal browns and rainbows. That fabulous sport continued all through the season right up to the back end.

Even the last four weeks of the 1978 season, in October, managed to produce an average of around 3,000 fish a week. The best seven day period, in August, turned up an incredible 5,150 fish from only 1,463 rods.

But things had settled down for the start of the 1979 season, especially through the effects of the winter. The opening week still fished amazingly well, with 2,775 visitors taking 7,769 trout in the first seven days.

But it was obvious that things had changed. For the bank men, at least, Bewl Bridge wasn't going to be the pushover it had proved to be in the past.

The fish were still well spread in the reservoir, but the freezing conditions had kept them low down in the deepest areas of the fishery. Boat men still had no trouble finding their limits, but the fish just were not interested in moving close inshore.

Limit bags were still by no means uncommon from the bank, but many more anglers took only a few fish — and even regulars bgan to learn what the word blank meant.

With fish staying well down, it was a case of sunk line fishing, with Black Lure, Sweeney Todd and Whisky Fly commanding the most respect. Towards the middle of the summer, fly hatches started appearing around the banks, at last giving bank men the odd rising fish to cast at.

But the fish were slow to respond in the still cool water — though the appearance of massive sedge hatches towards the end of June finally started the ball rolling.

Anglers in and around London itself enjoy great sport with Thames Water Authority fisheries — even in the heart of the city itself.

The 1978 season at Barn Elms, near Hammersmith, was very successful. Anglers fish three waters there, each water around 20 acres. One, the No 5 reservoir, was opened in 1978 for boat fishing only. It was so popular that the following year the authority had to double its boat fleet to cope with demand.

Another of the other waters is fly only, while any legal method is allowed on the third. The warm autumn of 78 kept fish and anglers active right into October.

The season for the 'any method' fishery was extended until December 21 at a reduced price, but not many people braved the cold and snow to take advantage.

1979 started well, with fish coming consistently on all three pools, including rainbows to 7lb — no brown trout are stocked in the waters.

The Thames Water Authority also has two waters at Walthamstow, one of them 'any method'. 1978 was the first year this 'any method' fishery was opened for trout, but it proved much better than the old water it had replaced — now a carp and tench fishery.

Anglers kept on visiting Walthamstow much later than in previous years, right up until the season ended in October.

The waters started slowly in 1979, despite a postponed opening date caused by repair and maintenance work. But by mid-season, they had yielded browns to 5lb 2oz and rainbows to well over 7lb.

The eagerly-awaited opening of Farmoor II, near Oxford, occurred in 1978 — and the patient anglers were rewarded with some incredible catches. Farmoor fished well right up until September, but then sport tailed off — though not before it had produced browns to 3lb and along list of big rainbows, topped by a six-pounder.

The Thames Water Authority were well pleased with their new baby. The water staged a repeat performance in 1979, despite a slow start because of the poor weather. By the halfway stage it had already topped the brown record with a 3lb 2oz fish, and the best rainbow of 1978 was nudged several times.

In contrast London's showpiece Queen Mother Reservoir, near Windsor, went through 1978 maintaining its reputation as a hard water to fish.

The boat-only concrete bowl did have its rewards, though, for perseverance, with a much bigger average class of trout than the other authority fisheries.

The fine autumn gave especially good sport to finish up with browns and rainbows topping the 6lb mark. Both those were beaten very quickly in 1979, with a 6½lb brown and a magnificent 8lb 3oz rainbow recorded by mid-season.

On average, the start was slow. Those deep sections of Queen Mother took a long time to warm up and it was lure fishing on a slow sink line all through.

The reservoir is very exposed, and those harsh Spring winds curtailed a lot of boat activity.

An angler in action at Barn Elms — one of the Thames Water Authority's many reservoirs.

Reservoir Figures:

Bewl Bridge

Total catch 1978	Total to June 1979	Best brown 1978	Best brown 1979	Best rainbow 1978	Best rainbow 1979
99,304	29,757	4lb 12oz	3lb 2oz	5lb 11oz	7lb 9oz

Barn Elms

Total catch 1978	Total to June 1979	Best brown 1978	Best brown 1979	Best rainbow 1978	Best rainbow 1979
21,384	12,723	—	—	5lb	7lb

Walthamstow

Total catch 1978	Total to June 1979	Best brown 1978	Best brown 1979	Best rainbow 1978	Best rainbow 1979
16,748	6,671	4lb	5lb 2oz	7lb 4oz	7lb 11oz

Farmoor

Total catch 1978	Total to June 1979	Best brown 1978	Best brown 1979	Best rainbow 1978	Best rainbow 1979
32,370	14,909	3lb	3lb 2oz	6lb	5lb 13oz

Queen Mother

Total catch 1978	Total to June 1979	Best brown 1978	Best brown 1979	Best rainbow 1978	Best rainbow 1979
15,967	6,046	6lb	6lb 8oz	6lb 2oz	8lb 3oz